STUDENT EATS

RACHEL PHIPPS

CONTENTS

Introduction 6

Essential Equipment 8

Notes on the Core Ingredients 14

Useful Storecupboard
Ingredients 16

BREAKFAST 18

Get Ahead 20

Hot & Under 15 Minutes 28

Eggs 31

Pancakes & Sweet Things 36

Brunch 42

LUNCH 48

Salads 50

Sandwiches, Wraps &
Things on Toast 62

Leftovers & Light Bites 69

Hot & Under 15 Minutes 82

SOLO DINNERS 86

Pasta 88

Soups 96

Weeknight Wonders 99

Better Than Takeaway 110

FOOD FOR FRIENDS 114

Dinner for Two 116

Feasts 124

SOMETHING SWEET 142

Cakes, Cookies & Snacks 144

Puddings 154

DRINKS 168

MEAL MATHS 178

Take One Recipe 179

Using Everything Up 182

Storecupboard Meals 183

Food for Friends 184

Special Occasions 186

Three Meals for Under £10 187

Index 188

INTRODUCTION

I can remember clearly the afternoon my parents dropped me off at halls for my first year of university. I can remember my father trying to cram all of my bags and boxes into one ride of the lift, and my mother making my bed for me because she knew that I'd always hated doing it.

I can also remember the first box I unpacked the moment my parents had left. As I found homes for the battered pots and pans I'd inherited from my aunt's student days and for the bags of pasta and rice I'd been sent away with, I was absolutely terrified.

What worried me the most about moving away from home and starting university was that I wasn't going to be able to feed myself the fresh, healthy and pretty much 100% homemade food I was used to at home on a student budget. I was scared that I would run out of money for fresh food and have to start living off the student stereotype of packet meals, jarred sauces and bowls of 40p rice. It was in my efforts to avoid this bleak eventuality that I found my love of food and cooking.

I started writing a fashion blog while I was still at school. It was a space where I could share my photos and writing with the world. Therefore, it seemed natural to me to photograph and share the cheap, fresh and easy meals I'd started producing in my student kitchen. After a little while, everyone, from my best friend to total strangers, was telling me how much they'd enjoyed one dish or another.

I spent the second year of my degree studying abroad in California. It was in Los Angeles that I really stopped writing so much about clothes and make up, and started getting braver and bolder about creating my own dishes. I spent the holidays, when I had the kitchen to myself, perfecting some of my favourite recipes.

I WAS SCARED THAT I WOULD RUN OUT OF MONEY FOR FRESH FOOD AND HAVE TO START LIVING OFF THE STUDENT STEREOTYPE OF PACKET MEALS, JARRED SAUCES AND BOWLS OF 40P RICE.

My kitchen table in America was where I first started to imagine what a cookbook written for students like me could look like.

Fast-forward almost 5 years after that first day of student life and here is the book I wish I'd had back then. A book full of the sorts of recipes that you'd want to throw together after a packed day of lectures, or the morning after the night before. The most important thing to me when I was writing this book was also to make sure that it is a 'student' cookbook in name, budget and simplicity only.

SOMETHING BRIGHT, FRESH AND DELICIOUS, OR WARM, COSY AND COMFORTING, DOESN'T HAVE TO BE EXPENSIVE, DIFFICULT OR TIME INTENSIVE TO CREATE.

I hope you'll enjoy cooking from this book long after graduation. I wanted the recipes to have more in common with the dishes you'd find in a 'grown-up' cookbook, rather than some of the other student titles out there.

Writing my blog, I've had countless comments and emails from readers with busy lives and a tight budget, who have recently started their first jobs, have families to feed or who just want to eat well without spending all of their time in the kitchen. This book is for all of those people, too.

Looking away from my own student experience crammed into shoebox east London flats, I took a great interest in other student kitchens when I visited my friends. While I never really had the space to have people round for dinner, it could be different for you. In this book you'll find recipes that would easily feed a crowd from the kitchen of a sprawling student house, such as my friend's in

Nottingham, along with quick, two-person dishes that would be perfect when it is your night to cook, such as my best friend's cosy south London two-bed.

Everything else aside, the one thing I hope you will take away from this book, if you don't already have it, is a love of good food. Something bright, fresh and delicious, or warm, cosy and comforting, doesn't have to be expensive, difficult or time intensive to create. Remember that, and I promise you that you'll be prepared for life in a way that no university lecture or seminar will be able to teach.

ESSENTIAL EQUIPMENT

When you are short of money and space, and if you've never set up your own kitchen before, it is hard to know what to buy that you'll get the most use out of, and what items will get used only once or twice. There is no point investing in things that will just find their way to the back of the cupboard to gather dust.

I've divided the equipment you'll need to make all of the recipes in this book into two categories: kitchen essentials and items that are only essential if you gravitate more towards certain types of cooking. A muffin tin may be essential to a baker, and a wok to someone who loves a good stir-fry, but others may not get much use out of them.

The assumption is that you'll have already purchased plates, glasses, mugs and cutlery. I'm also assuming that you have a kettle, toaster, microwave and an oven with a grill in it, and a hob on top. If you're using a fan oven, drop the cooking temperature by 10 or 20 degrees depending on your oven.

KITCHEN ESSENTIALS

Knives

I cannot emphasise enough the importance of a couple of good, sharp kitchen knives. Ignore those cheap knife blocks marketed to students, full of knives that can barely cut, and invest in just two good ones. Knives that are not sharp are dangerous. I still have no idea how I made it to my 10am Medieval Literature seminar half an hour after passing clean out on the kitchen floor after cutting myself with a blunt knife while making breakfast one morning.

Choose one large, long knife, and one slightly smaller knife. You may think that one will do, but if you're cooking raw meat or fish, it is such a bother having to keep on washing up your knife in the middle of cooking.

If you can stretch to it, one knife I wish I had as a student was a good bread knife. You can use the serrated edge to cut most vegetables, and it will be a godsend when you come to slice tomatoes or a crusty loaf of bread.

Chopping Boards

Choose at least two large chopping boards: it's important to have a separate board for chopping raw meat and with two boards you don't have to stop and wash up halfway through cooking.

Pots and Pans

For cooking on the hob, usually it is cheaper to buy a nest of three saucepans: small, medium and large. However, if you're buying them separately, every recipe in this book can be made with just a medium and a large saucepan. Wherever a small one is called for, you can get away with using a medium pan instead. It does not matter if your pans don't have lids; just sit a baking tray on top and weigh it down with something heavy.

You will need a medium and a large frying pan, both of these preferably non-stick. A little one would be good, too, for things like single-serving crêpes, but it is not essential; just use the medium pan instead when a smaller pan is called for.

A wok is by no means a kitchen essential, but you may want to invest in one if you like Asian cooking. I also use my wok to make the fillling for fajitas in as it is roomier than my biggest frying pan. I had a flatmate from Hong Kong in third year who always made spaghetti bolognese in hers.

Sieve

Pick up a cheap plastic one. The amount of mess you make trying to drain the water away from a pan of pasta or rice without one is not worth saving a pound or two.

Baking Trays

While I like to have an assortment, you can get away with owning just one large, non-stick tray with a generously lipped edge. You'll be able to bake cookies on this in batches, roast vegetables on it and use it as a base for baking pieces of fish and the like.

Baking Dishes

In many instances I'll call for an ovenproof dish for baking anything from baked bean and egg pots to chicken pies and quiches. I'd recommend picking up something cheap of about the right size when you need it to build a collection of three or four different shapes and sizes, and then making do with the nearest approximate for any given recipe.

Measuring Spoons, Weighing Scales and Measuring Jugs

While for some recipes you can't really do without weighing scales, for a lot of the recipes in this book all you'll need is a set of measuring spoons. I'm pretty reliant on mine. If you don't own scales, a measuring jug is also great for volumes of liquid more than 15ml (1 tablespoon).

You can get a good pair of inexpensive scales on the high street or online. Any set of scales is better than nothing, but if I had to tell you outright to invest in one piece of kit for your kitchen, I'd send you out to buy a £10–15 pair of digital scales. They're an investment, yes, but if you measure everything out exactly, following pretty much any recipe, you'll have reduced your chances of potential failure by at least 80% from the outset.

Mixing Bowl

You can get away with owning just one large mixing bowl for practically everything. You'll want it to be made out of heatproof glass so that you can easily melt butter and chocolate in it over a pan full of simmering water when you want melted chocolate to decorate a cake, or to whip up a pan of brownies.

Mixing Spoons and Wooden Spatulas

Hypothetically you can mix most things using a dessertspoon, but still I think a 50p wooden spoon ought to fall under the category of kitchen essentials. One or two wooden kitchen spatulas are also cheap as anything, and pretty much the best thing to toss anything around a wok or frying pan.

Juicer or Lemon Squeezer

It is next to impossible not to waste juice trying to squeeze a lemon or a lime without some sort of implement. A wooden or plastic squeezer is fine, but I like to use a two-part metal juicer, which catches all of the pulp and the seeds, allowing the juice to drip down into the tray below.

Cling Film, Tin Foil, Baking Parchment and Plastic Bags

These are what some people call kitchen extras, but what I call kitchen essentials. Cling film is not only great for wrapping and covering food, it makes a great tin liner for things like ice cream terrines and refrigerator bars. Tin foil, I think, sometimes does a better job of lining a tin for things like brownies than baking parchment does. Squares of parchment make great impromptu muffin cases, and parchment is my favourite thing to bake salmon on as it stops the skin sticking to the baking tray.

I like large plastic bags for freezing leftover portions of food, and to marinate things in the fridge overnight. Buy a roll of gusseted bags, as you can fit more into them.

Grater

Your grater is another item that I'd recommend you spend a little more on to ensure you get something sharp.

Can Opener and Bottle Opener

I don't think I need to tell any student that they'll need a bottle opener with a beer attachment for university, but make sure you get a good-quality one. I remember all too well the evening I was writing the introduction to my dissertation and I had to call home to brainstorm ideas for how to extract the cork from a bottle of wine in which the corkscrew had snapped off and embedded itself in the cork while I was trying to open it.

In that vein, cheaper tins of food don't always have a ring pull, so don't forget a can opener. Also, be sure you actually know how to use it without the risk of losing a finger.

LITTLE EXTRAS

Garlic Crusher

For most of the recipes in this book, all you need to do is to peel and finely chop garlic. For the few recipes where crushed garlic is preferable, I've explained how to make a garlic paste by sprinkling finely chopped garlic with a little bit of salt, and drawing the flat edge of a large, sharp knife across it. However, if you use garlic in a large number of recipes, like I do, you'll save a lot of time by investing in a good hand-held crusher.

Vegetable Peeler

You could always use a knife, but I've found that a good vegetable peeler saves time. You can also use it to make ribbons of cucumber or carrot for salads.

Rolling Pin

A rolling pin certainly makes it easier to roll out pastry to make pie or some shortbread biscuits, but you can also get the job done using a wine bottle; just make sure it is either unopened or a screw top filled with water to lend it some weight.

Whisk

For most recipes in this book, you can get away with whisking with a fork. However, if you're playing with egg whites for something like a Dutch baby pancake, only a balloon whisk will get the job done. If you're hell bent on making something like a meringue in your student kitchen, get online and order an inexpensive electric whisk, because life is really too short to do it by hand.

Flexible Spatulas

While you can flip pancakes carefully using a knife, wooden spatula or a spoon, I have a flexible, fish slice-type spatula that I'd be lost without. The sort of spatula you can use to scrape away any leftover juices from a one-pan chicken roast, or the cake batter from the mixing bowl, would also be a useful addition.

Scissors

There is nothing that scissors can cut that a kitchen knife can't, but sometimes they're quicker and faster for things like quickly chopping rashers of raw bacon, which are surprisingly difficult to slice unless your knife is very, very sharp.

Stick Blender

The majority of the soups in this book are smooth, and for this you'll need an inexpensive electric stick blender. I would have been lost without mine as a student as I used to make soup out of any vegetables I had left over. You probably won't use it at all, however, if you're not a soup person.

Cake Tins

If you make muffins, cupcakes or Yorkshire puddings with any semblance of regularity, it is worth investing in a muffin tin. Cupcake cases have a tendency to splay under the weight of the cake batter when baked without a tin to support them, resulting in unattractive, unevenly baked cakes.

A loaf tin is not only good for cakes, but for making things like ice cream terrines and refrigerator bars, too. All of the recipes in this book use a 900g/2lb tin. Typically loaf tins come in two standard sizes, and this is the larger of the two.

Avid cake makers will obviously want to collect different tins to suit different bakes, but if you're the type of person who usually only throws together a cake when it is someone's birthday or for another special occasion, one round, deep, 20cm, preferably non-stick cake tin will do. If you don't want to buy a brownie pan, you can bake brownies in a well-lined or greased cake tin, too.

To make any tin non-stick without having to line it with foil or baking parchment, butter it really well and sprinkle it with flour, making sure the entire inside of the pan is well coated, including in all of the corners.

And if you bake a lot, whether large cakes or small bakes, you will need a wire rack for cooling.

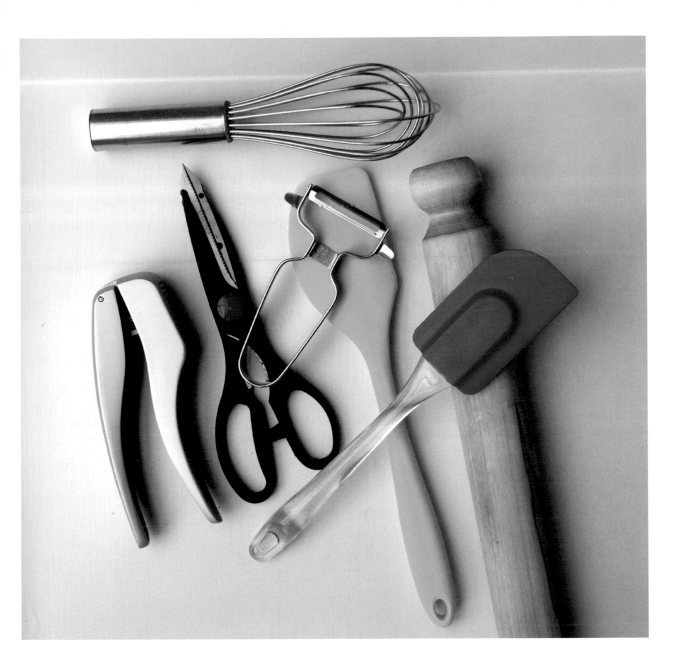

Roasting Tray

If you like to roast a bird at the weekend, or you're into things like chicken wings that require dousing in marinade before roasting in the oven, a deeper roasting tray (bonus points if it comes with a rack inside to rest your bird on), rather than just sticking to a lipped baking tray, may also be a helpful addition to your kitchen.

Cocktail Shaker

If you want to make cocktails at home, a shaker is by no means essential. A jam jar works perfectly well, but I must say that a proper shaker is worth the money if you make mix cocktails regularly. I just have a basic, three-part stainless-steel one, and I use it most weekends.

NOTES ON THE CORE INGREDIENTS

Throughout this book I've tried to give guidance and advice to help you choose the best ingredients for each recipe. For example, I always use large eggs in my cooking and baking, so I've listed any eggs in my ingredient lists as 'large' in every recipe. However, there are a few core ingredients that may be easy to overlook but which are worth a mention here. It is almost impossible to produce a good meal with poor ingredients, however basic, so make sure you get them right!

Cooking Oil

Throughout the book, I've used only two different types of cooking oils: light oil and extra virgin olive oil.

Extra virgin olive oil is what you should use when you're actually going to be tasting the oil, such as drizzled on toast or spooned into salad dressings. Good extra virgin can be a little pricey (though there are some good-value versions on the market) and doesn't last forever, so buy a small bottle. Supermarket own-brands are actually very good; just make sure the oil is marked as extra virgin, so you don't buy a blended oil by mistake.

When I refer to light oil, you could use any mild or flavourless oil you want. Which oil you choose has a lot to do with your cooking preferences. I always have a bottle of mild olive oil to hand. Vegetable and sunflower oils are very cheap and do the job perfectly, and if you do a lot of Asian cooking you might want to make groundnut your oil of choice.

You can also substitute other oils in a lot of my recipes. If you're roasting vegetables or chicken during the colder months, bright yellow rapeseed oil makes a wonderful addition. If you like the flavour, it is also great in salad dressings. Coconut oil has become really popular and is coming down in price. I adore the flavour and scramble my eggs in a couple of spoonfuls; you can substitute it anywhere you want to add its unique, slightly sweet flavour.

Salt and Pepper

It may sound a bit over the top that I've called for 'freshly ground sea salt and black pepper' in practically every recipe that includes seasoning, but I have a secret. If you look in the spice aisle in most supermarkets, for £1 to £2 you should be able to find plastic, pre-filled rock salt or sea salt grinders, and their black peppercorn counterparts. Typically, it takes me an entire academic year to get through one of these.

Some recipes in this book have 'sea salt' listed instead. I've asked you to use sea salt when you're actually going to be tasting salt as an ingredient in its own right. Choose a coarse sea salt; you should be able to get a good amount for under £1.

Finally, while I don't like to use table salt in cooking, when I've called for 'a pinch of salt' in baking recipes, table salt is what you should reach for. It is so cheap that there is no excuse not to pick up a container, but if you don't have room for yet another container of salt in your kitchen cupboard, just use sea salt. Throughout my second year I used sea salt in all of my baking; the world did not end.

I know having a couple of different salts in your kitchen sounds like overkill, but trust me: the way you salt your food dramatically changes the flavour more than any other ingredient.

Rice

All of the cooking times listed for brown rice in this book are for brown basmati rice. It does not matter what type of rice you buy; just stick to the listed weights, and check the back of the pack for cooking times.

Butter

While salted butter is good on toast, I use unsalted butter in all of my cooking, for the simple reason that it is easier to control the amount of salt in a dish, and therefore its flavour, by adding all of the salt yourself.

For ease, most butter packets have 15g, 25g or 50g measures marked on them, which provide a helpful guide to measuring butter without the need for weighing scales.

Milk

I use whole milk as standard, but you can substitute semi-skimmed or skimmed cows' milk in most of the recipes in this book. However, when it comes to baking, while the recipes will still work, you'll get the best results using whole milk.

Sugar

I use golden caster sugar as standard in my kitchen as it is unrefined and therefore better for you, and I like the slight caramel tone it lends to cakes and bakes. It is slightly more expensive than plain white, however, so this is down to personal preference.

The other sugar I always have to hand is soft light brown sugar. This is great in baking, and to add a deeper, burnt caramel flavour to dishes. If you have these two sugars in your cupboard, you can make practically anything. A third sugar you might need is icing sugar. Even if you're health conscious, white refined is best. It preserves the true colour of food colouring better, and has a more uniform flavour than its golden counterpart.

Vanilla Extract

I know a little bottle of vanilla extract looks expensive, but I promise you that a little will go a long way to enhancing the flavour of your bakes in a way that cheaper, artificial vanilla essence won't.

Cooking Chocolate

I've used a mixture of dark and plain chocolate in this book. However, you can use plain cooking chocolate (around 36% cocoa) for everything, if you prefer. Usually I buy just chocolate chips, ready to throw into cakes and cookie batters, or to melt without having to chop chocolate into small pieces. However, it is cheaper to buy a bar and break it up as you need it.

USEFUL STORECUPBOARD INGREDIENTS

After a few months of cooking for yourself, you will find out which items you always like to have to hand, and which ones you always seem to need to replace. However, to get you started, here are a few items I think any starter kitchen should be stocked with, and which I class as absolute essentials.

All of the ingredient lists in this book are split into two categories: storecupboard and fresh. If you buy everything on the list below the first time you go shopping, you will only need to buy fresh items when you're planning a meal.

light oil
extra virgin olive oil

white wine vinegar
red wine vinegar
balsamic vinegar

sea salt
black Peppercorn Grinder
table salt

dried oregano
dried chilli flakes
ground cumin
chilli powder

chicken stock cubes
vegetable stock cubes

worcestershire sauce
dark and light soy sauces
tabasco

dijon mustard
wholegrain mustard
light mayonnaise

nonpareille capers
anchovy fillets in olive oil
pesto
tinned chopped tomatoes

brown rice
pasta shapes
spaghetti, tagliatelle or linguini
egg noodles

white onions
red onions
garlic

vanilla extract
bicarbonate of soda
baking powder
cocoa powder
plain cooking chocolate
plain flour
golden caster sugar
runny honey

BREAK-FAST

GET AHEAD 20

HOT & UNDER 15 MINUTES 28

EGGS 31

PANCAKES & SWEET THINGS 36

BRUNCH 42

HOMEMADE GRANOLA WITH SPINACH, NATURAL YOGHURT & FRESH BERRIES

MAKES: 5 portions | **PREP TIME:** 10 minutes | **COOKING TIME:** 10–12 minutes

When I first saw granola served with spinach and yoghurt on the menu during my Study Abroad year in California, I could not understand how raw spinach could work as part of a breakfast dish. Yet if you were to blend all of the ingredients here into a smoothie, nothing would seem unusual. Served either way, it's a great combination.

You can use whatever you like in your granola, from different nuts and seeds to dried fruit; it is all down to personal preference. Also, while I enjoy soft berries such as strawberries and raspberries for breakfast, you can use anything you like or that is in season, from sliced apple and pomegranate seeds to grapefruit segments.

1. Preheat the oven to 150°C/300°F/Gas mark 2.

2. In a large bowl, whisk together the oil, 1 tablespoon of the honey, the maple syrup and vanilla extract. Stir in the oats, pumpkin seeds, almonds and coconut until everything is completely coated in the syrup mixture.

3. Line a large, flat baking tray with baking parchment and spread the oat mixture out across the tray. It does not matter if you have a few clumps, because this is how you get nice crunchy granola clusters.

4. Bake the granola for 10 to 12 minutes until it has started to go golden. Set the tray aside to cool completely; the granola will be soft when it comes out of the oven, but will crisp up and harden as it cools.

5. Portion out the yoghurt, spinach, granola and fresh fruit into soup bowls before drizzling with the remaining honey.

6. Store the granola in an airtight container. It should keep for at least 2 weeks.

STORECUPBOARD

1 tablespoon light oil

1½ tablespoons runny honey

1 teaspoon vanilla extract

FRESH

4½ tablespoons maple syrup

150g porridge oats

30g pumpkin seeds

40g blanched almond flakes

50g unsweetened desiccated coconut

3–4 generous spoonfuls of natural or Greek yoghurt

a small handful of baby spinach

a small handful of seasonal berries

FORCED RHUBARB & CARDAMOM BREAKFAST COMPOTE

MAKES: 6 portions | **PREP TIME:** 5 minutes | **COOKING TIME:** 10–15 minutes

I like long weekend breakfast and brunch projects, but actually eating something that is not a chocolate chip cookie (guilty!) when I'm in a hurry during the week is a challenge. One way I've found of combating this is to make up a bowl of compote to keep in the fridge. It is excellent spooned over fresh yoghurt (with a handful of Homemade Granola, page 20), oatmeal and even pancakes for more relaxed mornings.

Cardamom is one of my favourite spices. I sometimes replace the vanilla in the custard mix for a bread and butter pudding with a couple of cardamom pods. It adds a bit of perfume and an exotic Middle Eastern flavour to the rhubarb here, making this compote something extra special.

1. Wash the rhubarb, cut off the white bits at the bottom and any green at the top, and cut into 2cm chunks. Place the chunks in a medium saucepan along with the sugar, orange juice and the cardamom pods, lightly crushed under a heavy object (like the end of a rolling pin) to release the seeds.

2. Stir to combine, and cook over a high heat until the juice starts to boil. Stir, reduce the heat to medium and cover.

3. Leave to simmer for 10 to 15 minutes, stirring occasionally, until the rhubarb has broken down into a smooth compote. Add a bit more sugar if it tastes a little tart, and fish out the green cardamom husks and as many black seeds as you can find.

4. Let the compote cool to room temperature before you transfer to a bowl. Cover and keep it in the fridge for up to 5 days.

STORECUPBOARD

2 tablespoons golden caster sugar

FRESH

4 stalks of forced rhubarb

juice of 1 orange

4 green cardamom pods

HONEYED CARDAMOM-SOAKED APRICOTS WITH PISTACHIOS & GREEK YOGHURT

SERVES: 1 | **PREP TIME:** 5 minutes | **COOKING TIME:** 20 minutes

This is a great, make-ahead breakfast you can stash in the fridge when you know you've got an early start in the morning. You can also let it bubble away while you're making something else for dinner.

You can easily scale it up, but to make sure you get a good ratio of syrup to apricot, scale up your saucepan size too. For example, if you're doubling the mixture, use a medium saucepan, and if you're tripling it, use a large one. Make sure that the liquid is always just covering the apricots.

1. Combine the apricots, honey, orange juice and 150ml water in a small saucepan. Lightly crush the cardamom pods using the flat side of a large knife and add them to the pan.

2. Bring the mixture to the boil over a high heat, then reduce the heat to medium low. Allow the apricots to simmer away for 20 minutes. Leave to cool before transferring to a bowl, then covering and stashing in the fridge.

3. Remove the cardamom pods from the syrup and discard them. Serve the apricots spooned over Greek yoghurt and sprinkled with a small handful of pistachios. The apricots will keep for a couple of days in the fridge.

STORECUPBOARD

½ tablespoon runny honey

FRESH

8 dried apricots

juice of ½ orange

2 green cardamom pods

4 generous spoonfuls of Greek yoghurt

a small handful of shelled pistachios, roughly chopped

CHORIZO BAKED BEANS

MAKES: 6 portions | **PREP TIME:** 5 minutes | **COOKING TIME:** 45 minutes

Since making my own, I've never been able to eat tinned baked beans. Here the chorizo makes them a bit smokier and a bit more substantial in flavour. Even when I'm just cooking for myself, I like to make a big pan of these for a Sunday night supper on toast, perhaps with a fried egg, so there are then enough in the fridge for days when I need something a bit more hearty for breakfast. I also use them to make my Baked Egg & Homemade Baked Bean Pots (page 32), and a couple of spoonfuls are great with a full English.

1. Add the oil and the onion to a large heavy-based saucepan and set it over a medium heat. Once the onion starts to sizzle, cook for about 5 minutes until it starts to soften. Add the garlic and cook for another 2 minutes until the garlic has softened. Meanwhile, cut the chorizo into small cubes.

2. Add the chorizo to the pan and fry for 6 to 8 minutes until the oil has started to come out of the chorizo and it has gone a little crispy around the edges.

3. Open the beans into a sieve and rinse under a cold tap. Add them to the pan, along with the stock, tomatoes, oregano, Worcestershire sauce, mustard, balsamic vinegar, sugar and a good few grinds of salt and pepper. Stir well and reduce the heat to low. Allow to simmer without a lid for 30 minutes, stirring occasionally.

STORECUPBOARD

½ tablespoon light oil

I small onion, finely chopped

2 large garlic cloves, thinly sliced

200ml chicken stock (made with ½ stock cube)

2 x 400g tins chopped tomatoes

½ tablespoon dried oregano

½ teaspoon Worcestershire sauce

½ teaspoon Dijon mustard

½ teaspoon balsamic vinegar

a large pinch of golden caster sugar

freshly ground sea salt and black pepper

FRESH

8cm eating chorizo

2 x 400g tins cannellini beans

SMOKED SALMON BAGEL BREAKFAST CASSEROLE

SERVES: 2–3 | **PREP TIME**: 15 minutes, plus overnight chillling | **COOKING TIME**: 15 minutes

I love the breakfast 'casserole', an idea that hails from the American South Chunks of bread and all manner of different accompaniments are soaked in a wonderful eggy mixture. They are then baked together to yield a soft, chewy bottom and a wonderfully crunchy top.

Inspired by the smoked salmon and cream cheese bagels sold on Brick Lane at any time of the day or night (which were perfect for my late-night study sessions), I've given the American classic a slightly Yiddish twist with the addition of smoked salmon, cream cheese, red onions and vinegary capers.

I like all of the eggy goodness to have soaked into the bread, so I only use two eggs. However, if you'd like a slightly more set casserole with more discernible egg, use an extra egg and an additional 50ml of milk. You may have to bake the casserole for a few minutes more to ensure that the egg is set.

1. Butter an ovenproof baking dish so that the casserole does not stick to the sides.

2. Cut the bagels into small chunks and scatter them in the dish. It should be a snug fit, but comfortable enough to fit the other toppings.

3. Slice the red onion and tear the smoked salmon into small strips. Scatter these, along with the capers, over the bagel layer, tucking bits of salmon and onion into any gaps. Spoon the cream cheese into other gaps in even dollops.

4. Whisk together the eggs, milk and a generous amount of salt and pepper. Pour this evenly over the casserole and finish with another few grinds of salt and pepper over the top. Cover, and refrigerate overnight.

5. In the morning, preheat the oven to 200°C/400°F/Gas mark 6.

6. Take the casserole out of the fridge to bring it up to room temperature. Once the oven is up to temperature, bake the casserole for 15 minutes, until the top is crisp and the whole thing has puffed up a little.

7. Serve with a glass of orange juice and a green salad.

STORECUPBOARD

¼ red onion

4 teaspoons nonpareille capers

freshly ground sea salt and black pepper

FRESH

unsalted butter, for greasing the dish

3 bagels

2 slices of smoked salmon

cream cheese

2 large eggs

100ml milk

LEFTOVER BAKED INDIAN-SPICED POTATOES WITH TOMATO, EGG & CORIANDER

SERVES: 1 | **PREP TIME:** 5 minutes | **COOKING TIME:** 5 minutes

STORECUPBOARD

a splash of light oil

freshly ground sea salt and black pepper

FRESH

a generous handful of leftover Indian Spiced Potatoes (page 83)

4 cherry tomatoes, halved

1 large egg

a small handful of fresh coriander, roughly torn

This is another dish that is fantastic for using up leftovers. It is also super-quick to throw together, so is perfect to make in the morning before class.

Alternatively, if you've agreed to make weekend brunch for a couple of friends, you can make an entire batch of Indian Spiced Potatoes (page 83), up the amount of tomatoes and fresh coriander, and use one egg per person in the largest frying pan you have. Carry the whole thing to the table and serve with a pitcher of Cheat's Vegetable Juice Bloody Mary (page 42).

1. Heat a splash of oil in a small (preferably non-stick) frying pan over a medium-high heat. Once the oil is shimmering, add the potatoes and the tomatoes and stir briefly. Create a well in the middle and crack in the egg.

2. Reduce the heat to medium and cook until the egg is set. Remove the pan from the heat. Season well with freshly ground sea salt and black pepper and sprinkle generously with fresh coriander. Transfer the egg and potato mixture onto a warm plate to serve.

CLASSIC SAVOURY EGGY BREAD

SERVES: 1 | **PREP TIME:** 5 minutes | **COOKING TIME:** 10 minutes

STORECUPBOARD

a dash of Worcestershire sauce

freshly ground sea salt and black pepper

a very generous glug of light oil

FRESH

1 large egg

1 tablespoon milk

6–8 x 4cm rounds of leftover baguette

You can make eggy bread with any stale, leftover bread, but I think it is best with leftover pieces of baguette. While the addition of Worcestershire sauce to the egg mixture is not traditional, I think it adds a subtle savoury boost to the proceedings. Feel free to leave it out if you prefer, or add a little more if you like the flavour.

Serve with grilled cherry tomatoes or some tomato ketchup, whichever takes your fancy. I'm a ketchup girl all the way!

1. Beat together the egg, milk, Worcestershire sauce and a very generous few grinds of sea salt and black pepper in a shallow dish. Add the bread rounds and leave to soak in the egg mixture for about a minute, before turning them over.

2. Heat the oil in a large (preferably non-stick) frying pan over a medium-high heat. Once the oil is shimmering, fry the bread rounds until golden on one side. Turn them over to cook on the other side until they're crisp and golden all over. Serve straight away.

CHICKEN LIVERS & ONIONS ON TOAST

SERVES: 2 | **PREP TIME:** 5 minutes | **COOKING TIME:** 15 minutes

I've always loved chicken livers, but I didn't start eating them for breakfast until I stopped making it home for dinner. I used to buy them on special offer and stash them in the freezer. I'd take a portion out to defrost with good intentions of making it back, but would end up cooking them in a rush before class the next morning after spending the evening in the pub instead.

For those of you who are slightly unsure about eating liver for breakfast, give it a go. Chicken livers are very cheap, super-delicious and cook really quickly.

I. Set a medium frying pan over a medium-high heat and melt the butter until it becomes frothy. Add the onion and fry for 5 minutes until it's soft and starting to go golden. Now is also the time to toast your bread.

2. Add the livers and cook for 6 to 7 minutes until they have started to brown on the outside, but are still slightly pink on the inside if you cut into one. Season generously with salt and pepper and serve spooned over the toast, sprinkled with chopped fresh parsley, if you happen to have any hanging around.

STORECUPBOARD

I large onion, thinly sliced

freshly ground sea salt and black pepper

FRESH

a very large knob of unsalted butter

4 slices of bread

400g chicken livers

a small handful of roughly chopped fresh parsley (optional)

SINGLE-SERVING SPICY BAKED EGGS IN TOMATO SAUCE

SERVES: 1 | **PREP TIME**: 5 minutes | **COOKING TIME**: 20 minutes

This is a total cheat's version of the Middle Eastern classic, which just so happens to be one of the easiest and most impressive savoury breakfasts you can make.

You can get more out of this recipe by doubling up on the sauce so you can use the leftovers from the fridge for 10-minute eggs any morning of the week. You can also triple or quadruple the whole thing to feed a few more of you.

1. Preheat the oven to 200°C/400°F/ Gas mark 6.

2. Add the garlic to a small, cold frying pan, along with a splash of light oil. Set over a medium heat. When the garlic has started to sizzle, add the tomatoes, spices, a pinch of sugar and a generous few grinds of salt and pepper. Allow to bubble for 5 minutes. Check you're happy with the seasoning. Add more salt if you think it is a little bland, and more sugar if it is too tart.

3. Transfer the sauce into a small, shallow baking dish. Crack the egg into the middle of the sauce and bake in the oven for 10 minutes until the egg has just set. Sprinkle with coriander just before serving with lots of hot toast.

STORECUPBOARD

1 large garlic clove, thinly sliced

a splash of light oil

½ x 400g tin chopped tomatoes

½ teaspoon dried chilli flakes

a pinch of golden caster sugar

freshly ground sea salt and black pepper

FRESH

¼ teaspoon sweet smoked paprika

1 large egg

roughly chopped fresh coriander, to serve

toast, to serve

BAKED EGG & HOMEMADE BAKED BEAN POTS

SERVES: 1 | **PREP TIME:** 5 minutes | **COOKING TIME:** 15 minutes

Inspired by a popular fast food joint serving 100% natural and homemade dishes, these deliciously simple baked bean pots are ready in the time it takes to get dressed in the morning. You can make these in any small ovenproof dish, or even in the bottom of a mug. While leftover homemade beans are best, you can always used the tinned variety, too.

1. Preheat the oven to 200°C/400°F/ Gas mark 6.

2. Fill a small ovenproof ramekin or pot three-quarters full with leftover baked beans. Crack an egg on top and season with salt and pepper. Bake for 15 minutes until the egg is just set. Serve with buttered toast.

STORECUPBOARD

freshly ground sea salt and black pepper

FRESH

a portion of leftover Chorizo Baked Beans (page 24)

1 large egg

buttered toast, to serve

GREEN EGGS & HAM

SERVES: 1 | **PREP TIME:** 5 minutes | **COOKING TIME:** 5 minutes

STORECUPBOARD

a splash of light oil

1 tablespoon pesto

freshly ground sea salt
and black pepper

FRESH

1 English breakfast
muffin

4 slices of ham
(see introduction,
below)

a large handful of rocket

2 large eggs

This is another brunch dish I had out at a restaurant, where I decided I could create a much more affordable version at home. It has become one of my favourites to eat in the spring, when I'm looking forward to the lighter eating of the warmer months, and I want everything to be fresh and green.

Use Parma ham or prosciutto here, if you can afford it. If not, wafer-thin ham would be equally delicious. You can use either jarred or fresh pesto here, whichever you have to hand.

1. Halve the muffin and toast it. Drape two slices of ham over each half and scatter with rocket.

2. Heat a small non-stick saucepan with a splash of oil over a medium-high heat. Fry both of the eggs until the whites are just set.

3. Top each half of the muffin with an egg. Mix a little water into the pesto to make it thin enough to drizzle, and drizzle it over each egg. Season the eggs with a generous few grinds of sea salt and black pepper.

CALIFORNIA SCRAMBLED EGGS

SERVES: 2 | PREP TIME: 5 minutes | COOKING TIME: 5 minutes

This is my favourite way to eat scrambled eggs in the morning. I've used good unsalted butter to scramble the eggs here, but you could also use 2 tablespoons of cold-pressed extra virgin coconut oil. However, coconut oil can be expensive, and good butter always makes excellent eggs.

This is a delicious way to use up leftover Pico de Gallo Salsa, if you've made a bowl to pair with Chicken Fajitas (page 126) or to top a baked potato.

1. Beat together the eggs with a generous few grinds of sea salt and black pepper. Slice the avocado and toast the bread. Leave the bread in the toaster to keep it warm while you scramble the eggs.

2. Set a small saucepan over a medium-high heat and melt the butter. Once the butter is frothy (or the coconut oil if, you're using it, is shimmering), add the eggs and stir constantly, scraping the bottom until you have a soft scramble.

3. Arrange the toast and the avocado on two plates and divide the eggs between them. Spoon over the salsa and finish with a few grinds of pepper.

STORECUPBOARD

freshly ground sea salt
and black pepper

FRESH

5 large eggs

1 large ripe avocado

4 slices of bread

a very large knob of
unsalted butter

4 tablespoons Pico de
Gallo Salsa (page 127)

DIPPY EGGS WITH ANCHOVY BUTTER SOLDIERS

SERVES: 1 | **PREP TIME:** 5 minutes | **COOKING TIME:** 5 minutes

You've got one of my favourite places to have brunch in London, Beagle in Hoxton, to thank for the inspiration for this stupidly simple and moreish anchovy butter, slathered on farmhouse soldiers and dunked into deliciously gooey eggs.

I like to buy anchovies packed in olive or sunflower oil rather than in salt, as I find it is easier to regulate the amount of salt in a dish this way.

1. Add the eggs to a vigorously boiling saucepan of water and boil for exactly 5 minutes to achieve the perfect set whites and runny yolks. Meanwhile, toast the bread to your liking, and mash the anchovies into the butter on a small plate until you'd made a smooth butter. Spread on the hot toast and slice into soldiers. Transfer the eggs to a pair of egg cups before digging in.

HOW TO BOIL THE PERFECT EGG

Boiled eggs are really easy to get right as long as you stick to the times below, which are for large eggs at room temperature, not cold from the fridge.

5 minutes – the perfect soft-boiled egg, with a hard white and runny yolk.

6 minutes – the perfect medium-boiled egg, with a hard white and yolk that is just set enough to slice for salads.

9 minutes – the perfect hard-boiled egg, with a hard white and a chalky yolk.

Make sure your saucepan of water is set over a very high heat and is at a rolling boil (which means it is very, very bubbly).

Sometimes your eggs, even if they're at room temperature, will crack when you place them in the boiling water. However, the easiest way to try and prevent this is to stop the egg shells cracking on the bottom of the pan. Do this by lowering each egg into the water using a large spoon.

STORECUPBOARD

2–3 anchovy fillets in olive oil

FRESH

2 large eggs

2 thick slices of bread

a very large knob of unsalted butter, at room temperature

OVERNIGHT BUTTERMILK PANCAKES

MAKES: 5–6 pancakes | **PREP TIME**: 5 minutes, plus overnight chilling (optional) | **COOKING TIME**: 30 minutes

This basic buttermilk American-style pancake batter is the starting point for the perfect weekend breakfast. You don't have to make the batter ahead and leave it in the fridge overnight, but I find that it does not affect the pancakes at all if you do, and it will help save time in the morning.

Serve with whichever fresh fruits, chopped nuts or syrups you fancy. You can make these into blueberry pancakes by throwing a few fresh berries on top of each pancake in the pan before you flip them.

1. Combine the sugar, bicarbonate of soda, salt and flour in a medium bowl.

2. In a separate bowl or jug, whisk together the egg and buttermilk. Gradually whisk this into the flour mixture until you have a smooth batter. If you choose to refrigerate the batter at this point, cover the bowl with cling film before stashing it in the fridge.

3. When you are ready to cook, heat a medium or large (preferably non-stick) frying pan over a medium heat. If the pan is non-stick, you'll only need a splash of oil to cook with. If it isn't non-stick, you may need a bit more.

4. Once the oil is hot, spoon two to three spoonfuls of batter into the pan. Cook the pancake for 5 minutes, flipping it over once the edges have started to brown and the batter has started to bubble up in the middle of the pancake. Keep warm while you cook the rest of the pancakes.

STORECUPBOARD

1½ tablespoons golden caster sugar

¼ teaspoon bicarbonate of soda

a pinch of salt

8 tablespoons plain flour

light oil

FRESH

1 large egg

140ml buttermilk (half a carton)

AUTUMN-SPICED BANANA PANCAKES

MAKES: 5–6 pancakes | **PREP TIME:** 10 minutes | **COOKING TIME:** 30 minutes

When life gives you a couple of brown, squishy bananas, you make banana bread. However, when you've only got one such banana to hand, clearly the most sensible option is to knock up a towering stack of banana-studded pancakes made with warming, autumn spices.

Serve with maple syrup, and a couple of handfuls of chopped nuts toasted in a hot, dry frying pan.

1. Combine the flour, sugar, baking powder, salt and spices in a medium or large bowl.

2. In a separate bowl, mash half the banana and slice the other half into thin slices (you want about two to three slices for each pancake). Whisk the egg, oil and buttermilk into the mashed banana. Gradually whisk the liquid mixture into the flour mixture until the batter is smooth.

3. Heat a medium or large, preferably non-stick, frying pan over a medium heat. If the pan is non-stick, you'll only need a splash of oil to cook with. If it isn't non-stick, you may need a bit more.

4. Once the oil is hot, spoon two to three spoonfuls of batter into the pan, to form one pancake, and place two to three slices of banana on top. Cook until the edges are slightly crisp and the batter starts to bubble up in the middle, then flip the pancake over to cook for another few minutes. You can cook two in the pan at a time if it is big enough.

5. Place the pancakes on a warm plate lined with kitchen paper while you cook the rest of the pancakes.

STORECUPBOARD

70g plain flour

1 tablespoon golden caster sugar

1 teaspoon baking powder

a pinch of salt

2 teaspoons light oil, plus a little extra for the pan

FRESH

½ teaspoon ground cinnamon

½ teaspoon ground ginger

1 large ripe banana

1 large egg

70ml buttermilk (quarter of a carton)

CLASSIC DUTCH BABY PANCAKE WITH LEMON & SUGAR

SERVES: 1 | **PREP TIME:** 10 minutes | **COOKING TIME:** 15 minutes

Baked pancakes are magical. What starts off as a regular batter puffs up around the edges like a Yorkshire pudding, rippling down in the middle into the densest, most glorious pancake you've ever eaten. I like to serve it with classic lemon and sugar, but the 15 minutes you have while the pancake is in the oven gives you plenty of time to dream up all manner of toppings.

You'll need a balloon whisk or an electric whisk for this recipe rather than using a fork to beat the ingredients together. A fork will not get enough air into the eggs.

1. Preheat the oven to 200°C/400°F/Gas mark 6.

2. Whisk the eggs and the sugar together using a balloon whisk or an electric whisk until the mixture is frothy and very pale in colour. Whisk in the flour, salt, milk and vanilla.

3. Melt the butter in a medium frying pan with an ovenproof handle over a very high heat. Once the butter has melted, swish the melted butter up the sides of the pan.

4. Pour the pancake batter into the middle of the pan, tipping the pan so that the batter covers the base in an even layer. Put the pan in the oven to bake for 15 minutes until the pancake is crisp, puffy and golden.

5. Serve with lemon wedges and a generous sprinkling of sugar.

STORECUPBOARD

1 tablespoon golden caster sugar, plus extra to serve

3 tablespoons plain flour

a large pinch of salt

1 teaspoon vanilla extract

FRESH

2 large eggs

5½ tablespoons whole milk

a very large knob of unsalted butter

lemon wedges, to serve

BLUEBERRY & OAT BREAKFAST MUFFINS

MAKES: 6 | **PREP TIME**: 10 minutes | **COOKING TIME**: 20 minutes

Muffins are among the easiest cakes to make, and the hardest to screw up. This makes them ideal for first thing in the morning! If you're looking for a sweeter, more sugary muffin, you need to turn to my Banana & Nutella Muffins (page 146).

These breakfast muffins only have a little bit of added sugar, and are instead packed with flavourful and energy-boosting seeds, blueberries and oats. They're perfect to start the day with, either by themselves when they're fresh and warm from the oven, or toasted and spread with salted butter the next morning.

1. Preheat the oven to 180°C/350°F/Gas mark 4.

2. In a mixing bowl, combine the flour, baking powder, salt, sugar, pumpkin seeds and blueberries.

3. In a separate bowl or jug, whisk together the buttermilk, oil and egg until smooth.

4. Stir the liquid mixture into the dry mixture until everything is just combined. It does not matter if you still have a few lumps of flour in the mix, but if you overmix the batter you'll get tough muffins.

5. Spoon the mixture into six paper muffin cases placed in a muffin tin, if you have one. Sprinkle the top of each muffin with porridge oats and bake the muffins for 20 minutes.

6. Remove the muffins from the tin and allow them to cool on a wire rack for a few minutes before eating.

STORECUPBOARD

130g plain flour

1 teaspoon baking powder

a pinch of salt

2 tablespoons golden caster sugar

50ml light oil

FRESH

a generous handful of pumpkin seeds

2 large handfuls of fresh blueberries

100ml buttermilk

1 large egg

a handful of porridge oats

BREAKFAST GRITS WITH STRAWBERRIES & MAPLE SYRUP

SERVES: 1 | **PREP TIME:** 5 minutes | **COOKING TIME:** 15 minutes

When it is freezing cold outside a rich and creamy bowl of polenta makes a great accompaniment for practically anything Italian and with a tomato base, such as my Sausage Bolognese (page 134). However, I also love it for an indulgent winter breakfast, topped off with a few strawberries and a generous glug of maple syrup.

Different polenta brands take slightly different times to cook. Make sure you have a little extra water to hand, because if your polenta does take a little longer to get soft and smooth, you'll be needing to add it splash by splash. However, don't buy quick-cook polenta, as it is not suitable here.

1. Combine a very large pinch of sea salt and 180ml water in a small saucepan and bring to the boil over a high heat. Reduce the water to a simmer and add the polenta. Keep stirring until all of the water has been absorbed and the polenta is thick and hard to stir.

2. Add the milk and butter and stir again until the polenta is thick and the right consistency for you; this is down to personal preference. Season generously with salt and pepper. If you taste the polenta and it is gritty rather than smooth, add a bit more water and stir until it is all absorbed.

3. Spoon the polenta into a warm bowl, top with the strawberries, maple syrup and a generous few grinds of black pepper.

STORECUPBOARD

freshly ground sea salt and black pepper

FRESH

40g yellow polenta

120ml milk

a very large knob of unsalted butter

6-8 strawberries, hulled and sliced

a generous drizzle of maple syrup

STRAWBERRY & RICOTTA BREAKFAST TOAST WITH LEMON HONEY

SERVES: 1 | **PREP TIME:** 5 minutes

This super-quick and easy breakfast toast is great for using up leftovers. The last couple of strawberries from the punnet taste great on top of the last few scrapings from a tub of ricotta, and the juice from the last quarter of a lemon really brightens up the toppings for a thick toasted slice of a slightly stale loaf.

I. Toast the bread while you prepare the rest of your ingredients. In a small dish, mix together the lemon juice and the honey. Slice the strawberries.

2. Pile the ricotta onto the toast, followed by the strawberry slices. Drizzle with the honey and lemon mixture, and finish with a few generous grinds of black pepper.

STORECUPBOARD

I tablespoon runny honey

freshly ground black pepper

FRESH

I thick slice of farmhouse bread

½ tablespoon lemon juice

4–5 strawberries, hulled

60g ricotta

CHEAT'S VEGETABLE JUICE BLOODY MARY

SERVES: 1 | **PREP TIME**: 5 minutes

The very best Bloody Marys are made with a range of different vegetable and spice flavours, making for a more complex drink. A cheat's way of achieving this is to use vegetable juice rather than tomato juice.

This recipe serves one, so it can be easily scaled up to make a jugful if you're throwing a weekend brunch party.

1. Add all of the ingredients except for the celery stick to a large jam jar with a lid that seals very well. Make sure the jar is sealed, shake really well and pour into a tall glass, garnishing with the celery stick. Alternatively, mix everything up together in the glass until combined using a very long spoon.

STORECUPBOARD	FRESH
¼ teaspoon Tabasco	80ml vodka
¼ teaspoon Worcestershire sauce	1 tablespoon lemon juice
a few grinds of sea salt and black pepper	160ml vegetable juice
	a small handful of ice cubes
	a leafy celery stick (optional), to garnish

HANGOVER-CURE MEXICAN CHILAQUILES

SERVES: 1 | **PREP TIME:** 5 minutes | **COOKING TIME:** 15 minutes

I know that with my British passport and all I'm supposed to fly the flag for the good old full English. However, if you ask me, the nation that produces the very best breakfasts is Mexico. My favourite of all the corn- and salsa-heavy Mexican breakfast dishes? Chilaquiles – a breakfast of leftovers.

In that vein, the measurements here are just a rough guide. The idea is to use up leftover Mexican ingredients from making something like Chicken Fajitas (page 126) the night before.

You can find tins of black beans in the ethnic foods section of most supermarkets. Red kidney beans would make a good substitute.

1. Preheat the oven to 200°C/400°F/Gas mark 6.

2. Use scissors to cut up the tortilla into pieces the size and shape of tortilla chips, and spread across a baking tray. Bake in the oven for 5 minutes until slightly golden and crispy. Leave to cool on the baking tray.

3. Heat a splash of oil in a medium (preferably non-stick) frying pan over a medium heat. While the pan is heating up, thinly slice the red onion and radish. Fry the onion until soft. Add 4 teaspoons of the salsa and cook for about a minute, before stirring in the black beans.

4. Add the baked tortilla chips to the pan and stir in as much as you can until the tortilla chips are partially coated in salsa and beans, and they have started to go soft in a few places.

5. Make a shallow well in the middle of the pan and crack in the egg. Cook for about 5 minutes until the egg is set. Season the whole pan with salt and pepper and drizzle with the remainder of the salsa. Scatter with fresh coriander and sliced radish and slide the contents of the pan onto a plate. Serve with sliced avocado and a fresh lime wedge on the side.

STORECUPBOARD

a splash of light oil

¼ red onion

freshly ground sea salt and black pepper

FRESH

1 large flour tortilla

1 large radish

6 teaspoons Pico de Gallo Salsa (page 127)

5 tablespoons tinned black beans

1 large egg

a small handful of fresh coriander, roughly chopped

1 small avocado, sliced

1 lime wedge

SMOKED SALMON LATKES WITH LEMON CRÈME FRAÎCHE, CHOPPED RED ONION & CAPERS

SERVES: 2 | **PREP TIME:** 20 minutes | **COOKING TIME:** 20 minutes

This is the perfect fancy brunch for two. The classic Jewish potato latke has been gussied up with thin strips of smoked salmon, which gently cook and infuse the surrounding potato with wonderfully rich flavour. A little bit of salmon also goes a long way here, so use the rest of the packet to make a round or two of sandwiches.

1. Add the white onion, garlic and a splash of oil to a small frying pan and set over a medium heat. Cook the onion and the garlic until the onion is soft and starting to go golden, then remove them from the heat.

2. While you're frying the onion, coarsely grate the potato. Mix with a generous pinch of sea salt in a small bowl and set aside.

3. Beat together the eggs, flour, baking powder and a generous few grinds of black pepper to make a thick paste. Stir in the cooked onion and garlic.

4. Squeeze any excess liquid out of the grated potato over the sink in small handfuls and stir it into the onion and egg mixture. Slice the salmon into thin strips and stir them into the mixture too.

5. Heat a generous glug of oil in a large frying pan over a medium-high heat. Fry a couple of spoonfuls of the potato mixture at a time for a few minutes on each side until they are golden. As you're cooking in batches (you should get about 8 latkes), keep the rest of the latkes hot on a warm plate lined with kitchen paper to soak up any excess oil from frying.

6. While you're making the latkes, finely chop the red onion and leave it to soak in a small bowl of cold water. This will take the bite out of the raw onion. Meanwhile, mix the lemon juice into the crème fraîche.

7. To serve, pile the latkes up in two stacks, topping each one with a dollop of the lemon crème fraîche, capers and chopped red onion, drained and dried on a piece of kitchen paper first.

STORECUPBOARD

I small white onion, finely chopped

I large garlic clove, finely chopped

light oil

sea salt and freshly ground black pepper

2 tablespoons plain flour

½ teaspoon baking powder

3 slices of smoked salmon

¼ red onion

I tablespoon nonpareille capers

FRESH

I large baking potato, peeled

2 large eggs

juice of ¼ lemon

4 tablespoons crème fraîche

FULL ENGLISH BREAKFAST QUICHE

SERVES: 6 | **PREP TIME**: 20 minutes | **COOKING TIME**: 50 minutes

STORECUPBOARD

freshly ground sea salt and black pepper

FRESH

2 sausages

4 rashers of streaky bacon, chopped (I find it much easier using scissors)

5–6 chestnut mushrooms, thickly sliced

2 large eggs

2 egg yolks

1 x 150ml pot single cream

50ml milk

unsalted butter, for greasing the dish

12 cherry tomatoes

1 x 320g shortcrust pastry sheet

This quiche is great for lunch served with a side salad. However, I like it best as the perfect centrepiece to a lazy weekend brunch, made the night before.

If you don't have a pie or tart dish for your quiche, use whatever shallow ovenproof pan you can find with sides at least 4cm high and big enough to take all of your quiche filling.

After making your pastry case, you can make jam tarts by cutting the scraps into small circles, pressing them into the holes of a muffin tin and spooning a teaspoon or two of jam into the mini pastry cases. Bake them with your quiche until the pastry is golden; this will take less time than the quiche takes to cook.

1. Preheat the oven to 200°C/400°F/Gas mark 6.

2. Using a sharp knife, poke a few holes in each sausage so a lot of the water and fat comes out of them while they are cooking. Cook for 20 minutes. Once they are cooked through, leave them to cool.

3. Reduce the oven temperature to 180°C/350°F/Gas mark 4. If you're using a glass or metal dish to bake your quiche in, also put a baking tray in the oven to heat up. By cooking your quiche on this hot metal tray, you're less likely to get a soggy bottom.

4. Heat a large frying pan over a medium-high heat and add the bacon and the mushrooms together without any oil. Fry for about 5 minutes until the mushrooms are soft and the bacon has started to brown. Transfer from the pan to a plate lined with a couple of sheets of kitchen paper to soak up as much excess fat as possible. Slice the sausages into small pieces and leave them to drain on the plate, too.

5. While the bacon and mushrooms are frying, whisk together the eggs, egg yolks, cream, milk and a generous few grinds of salt and pepper to make the quiche filling.

6. Grease your dish generously with butter. If your pastry sheet is just that little bit too small to line the dish, sprinkle a clean work surface with flour and, using a rolling pin (or a bottle of wine!), roll it out a little thinner. Slide the dish under the pastry sheet to help line it without tearing the pastry, and push the pastry into the edges of the dish. If it does tear, don't worry! You can easily patch the pastry case with scraps from around the edges; the patches will get covered up with filling anyway.

7. To tidy up your pastry case, lift the dish up in the air and, using a very sharp knife, carefully slice any excess pastry from around the edges. By lifting your dish into the air you're making sure you cut at an angle that prevents the pastry from shrinking too much in the oven.

8. Sprinkle the mushroom, bacon and sausage mixture evenly across the bottom of the pastry case and arrange the cherry tomatoes evenly over the top. Pour over the quiche mixture and bake in the oven for 25 minutes until the pastry is golden and the quiche mixture has set and started to brown. Allow to cool for at least 10 minutes before serving.

LUNCH

SALADS..50

SANDWICHES, WRAPS
& THINGS ON TOAST..........................62

LEFTOVERS & LIGHT BITES.............69

HOT & UNDER 15 MINUTES............82

PEARL BARLEY, POMEGRANATE & PISTACHIO SALAD

SERVES: 2 | **PREP TIME:** 20 minutes | **COOKING TIME:** 30–40 minutes

STORECUPBOARD

freshly ground sea salt and black pepper

2 teaspoons extra virgin olive oil

FRESH

150g pearl barley

1 tablespoon pomegranate molasses

2 handfuls of shelled pistachios, roughly chopped

2 generous handfuls of pomegranate seeds

a large handful of fresh flat-leaf parsley, finely chopped

a large handful of fresh mint, finely chopped

Always buy a whole pomegranate and remove the seeds yourself; little packs of pomegranate seeds are disproportionately expensive. Also, take care when you're choosing pistachios. You want the shelled variety with no added salt. Some shops sell the same weight of nuts for more money in the snacks aisle, so look in the whole foods and baking aisles.

1. Place the pearl barley in the largest saucepan you have and cover with a couple of inches of cold water. You need to use a large saucepan for cooking even a small amount of pearl barley, as it froths up a lot while it is cooking. Set it over a high heat and bring to the boil. Let it cook for 30 to 40 minutes until the barley is tender, skimming the scum off the top of the cooking water halfway through. Keep an eye on it during cooking to make sure you don't need to add any more water to stop the barley drying out.

2. Drain the barley and rinse off any excess stickiness under a cold tap. This will also cool the barley down, ready to be made into a salad. Shake off as much excess water as you can, and rinse out the saucepan before tipping the barley back in. Add all of the salad ingredients, a generous seasoning of freshly ground sea salt and black pepper, and stir well until everything is combined. Taste a little, to make sure you've added enough salt and pepper. You can add more molasses too, if you think it needs a bit more tang, and a bit more oil if you think it's too dry.

GOOD GREEN COUSCOUS

SERVES: 2 | **PREP TIME**: 10 minutes | **COOKING TIME**: 5 minutes

STORECUPBOARD

extra virgin olive oil

freshly ground sea salt
and black pepper

FRESH

125g couscous

¼ cucumber, peeled
and cut into small
chunks

4 spring onions,
trimmed and sliced

2 large handfuls of
sugar snap peas, sliced

a large handful of fresh
coriander, finely
chopped

juice of ½ lemon

I love how stupidly quick it is to make couscous. For some reason, when I imagine a big bowl of couscous, I want it to have lots of fresh greens and lots of crunch. I also want it to improve over time, which is what this couscous salad does. So while it will taste great when you've just made it, this is one of those dishes you'll get excited about having stashed away in the fridge ready for the next day.

1. Combine the couscous, 200ml boiling water and 1 tablespoon of olive oil in a large bowl and cover with cling film. Leave to steam and absorb the liquid (about 5 minutes) while you prepare the rest of the salad.

2. Fluff up the couscous with a fork and mix in the chopped vegetables and herbs, followed by the lemon juice. Season to taste with freshly ground salt and pepper, and loosen with a little more olive oil if you think it needs it.

WARM LEFTOVER ROAST CHICKEN HONEY MUSTARD PASTA SALAD

SERVES: 1 | **PREP TIME:** 5 minutes | **COOKING TIME:** 12 minutes

This was one of my favourite weeknight suppers as a student. I pretty much have everything for this recipe in my fridge and in the kitchen cupboard at any time, and if you cook from this book regularly, you'll probably have the ingredients to hand, too.

If you don't have any leftover roast chicken, you can instead poach a chicken breast in a pan of simmering water for 20 minutes over a medium-low heat, before shredding it with a fork.

1. Put the pasta on to cook in a saucepan of salted boiling water over a high heat; cook until al dente, about 12 minutes.

2. Meanwhile, make the dressing by whisking together the mustard, honey, oil and vinegar.

3. Drain the pasta and return it to the saucepan. Pour over the dressing and add the tomatoes and chicken. Season well with salt and pepper, and stir until everything is coated in the honey-mustard dressing. Stir in the rocket before serving.

STORECUPBOARD

100g pasta shapes

1 tablespoon wholegrain mustard

½ tablespoon runny honey

1 teaspoon extra virgin olive oil

1 teaspoon white wine vinegar

freshly ground sea salt and black pepper

FRESH

a small handful of cherry tomatoes, halved

a large handful of shredded leftover Easy Lemon & Thyme Roast Chicken (page 138)

a large handful of rocket

COLD & CRUNCHY WINTER VEGETABLE NOODLE SALAD WITH ASIAN DRESSING

SERVES: 1 | **PREP TIME:** 15 minutes | **COOKING TIME:** 5–10 minutes

STORECUPBOARD

1 nest of egg noodles

FRESH

2 large handfuls of shredded curly kale

2 chestnut mushrooms, thinly sliced

3 Brussels sprouts, trimmed and shredded

2 spring onions, trimmed and thinly sliced

1 small carrot, peeled and thinly sliced

1 portion of Asian dressing (page 54)

This is a cold noodle salad designed for the cooler months, rather than the summertime. Winter vegetables like Brussels sprouts and curly kale are fantastic raw, especially doused in a punchy dressing.

1. Cook the noodles in a pan of salted boiling water over a high heat until tender. This usually takes 5 to 10 minutes, depending on the brand.

2. Drain the noodles, and run them under the cold tap for instant cold noodles. Shake off as much water as possible, and toss the noodles together with the vegetables and enough Asian dressing to ensure that everything is coated.

ASIAN PRAWN NOODLE SALAD WITH CRUNCHY GREENS

SERVES: 1 | **PREP TIME:** 5–10 minutes | **COOKING TIME:** 5–10 minutes

This is my ideal salad to make the night before and then pack up to eat on the go. You can use as much or as little of the Asian dressing on your salad as you want; it keeps very well in the fridge. I always have some made up to dress any number of different salads, bowls of rice or noodles.

I buy my edamame beans frozen, and I defrost a handful quickly to use in salads by running them briefly under warm water. You can also throw them still frozen into stir-fries. To safely defrost frozen cooked prawns, you need to run them under cold water.

1. Cook your chosen noodles as per the packet instructions.

2. Meanwhile, whisk together the soy sauce, mirin, honey, sesame oil and lime juice to make a dressing. Set aside while you prepare the vegetables.

3. Once the noodles are tender, rinse them under cold water to remove any excess starch and to create instantly cold noodles. Mix a drop of sesame oil into the noodles to stop them sticking together.

4. Transfer the noodles to a bowl or lidded plastic container, and arrange the vegetables and prawns on top. Drizzle over the dressing if you're eating straight away, otherwise store the salad, covered, in the fridge, along with the dressing in a separate sealed container, until you're ready to eat.

STORECUPBOARD

1½ teaspoons dark soy sauce

1 teaspoon runny honey

FRESH

100g soba, udon or egg noodles

1 teaspoon mirin

½ teaspoon toasted sesame oil, plus a drop for the noodles

½ teaspoon lime juice

1 large spring onion, trimmed and sliced on the diagonal

2 large radishes, trimmed and cut into 5mm slices

a large handful of pea shoots, lamb's lettuce or watercress

a small handful of edamame beans

a small handful of sugar snap peas, halved on the diagonal

¼ cucumber, peeled and cut into matchsticks

a small handful of cooked prawns

THE ONLY POTATO SALAD RECIPE YOU'LL EVER NEED

SERVES: 4 | **PREP TIME:** 10 minutes | **COOKING TIME:** 15–20 minutes

I created this potato salad to serve with barbecued sausages and griddled courgettes one summer evening using whatever I could find in the fridge. It has been my go-to summer side ever since. All of my friends have become familiar with it (and request it) whenever we have a beach barbecue, family-style summer dinner party or a picnic where we each bring a dish.

1. Place the potatoes in a large pan of salted cold water and set over a high heat. Bring the pan to the boil and cook the potatoes for 15 to 20 minutes. You'll know if they are done if you can easily push a knife into a potato.

2. Drain the potatoes and leave to cool. Halve the potatoes when they are cool enough to touch.

3. In a large mixing bowl, combine the mayonnaise, oil, mustard and vinegar with a very generous few grinds of salt and pepper.

4. Once the potatoes have cooled to room temperature, gently fold them into the mayonnaise mix until they are all well coated. Transfer them into a serving bowl and sprinkle with the spring onion pieces.

STORECUPBOARD

2 tablespoons light mayonnaise

2 teaspoons extra virgin olive oil

1 teaspoon wholegrain mustard

1 teaspoon white wine vinegar

freshly ground sea salt and black pepper

FRESH

10–15 baby new potatoes

1 large spring onion, trimmed and cut into 5mm slices

THE ONLY TUNA PASTA SALAD YOU'LL EVER NEED

SERVES: 2 | **PREP TIME:** 10 minutes | **COOKING TIME:** 12 minutes

I think everyone who loves a good tuna salad has spent time trying to perfect their own personal recipe; this is mine. I find the lemon zest and juice lift the dish, while the Greek yoghurt makes for a much lighter lunch dish, both in terms of health and flavour. Use this recipe as a starting point, and tweak it to make it your own.

1. Put the pasta on to cook in a saucepan of salted boiling water over a high heat; cook until al dente, about 12 minutes. Drain, and rinse under the cold tap until the pasta is cold. Shake the pasta in a sieve to try and remove as much excess water as possible.

2. Drain the tuna, and mix together with the mayonnaise, Greek yoghurt and mustard. Mix the red onion into the mayonnaise mixture, along with the sweetcorn, capers and lemon zest. Season generously with salt and pepper, and fold in the pasta shapes until they are well coated. Brighten up with a generous squeeze of lemon juice and check you are happy with the seasoning.

STORECUPBOARD

200g pasta shapes

3 tablespoons light mayonnaise

1 teaspoon Dijon mustard

¼ large red onion, finely chopped

1½ tablespoons nonpareille capers

freshly ground sea salt and black pepper

FRESH

1 x 112g tin tuna in spring water or brine

3 tablespoons light Greek yoghurt

2 large handfuls of tinned sweetcorn

zest of ½ lemon

a generous squeeze of lemon juice

SEAFOOD CITRUS SALAD RICE BOWL

SERVES: 1 | **PREP TIME:** 10 minutes | **COOKING TIME:** 25 minutes

This is a Californian-inspired rice bowl. If you defrost a couple of handfuls of mixed frozen seafood, you almost can't taste the difference from fresh once you've tossed them in a bright, zingy citrus dressing. Frozen seafood is also cheaper than fresh, and you don't have to worry about expiration dates.

1. Cook the rice in a pan of boiling water set over a high heat until the rice is tender. This should take about 25 minutes. Cook the rice like pasta, in a lot of water instead of in a set, measured amount. Using the absorption method is the easiest way to accidentally undercook, dry out or burn your rice.

2. While the rice is cooking, peel the grapefruit and the orange and chop the flesh into bite-sized pieces, reserving 1 teaspoon of grapefruit juice and 1 teapoon of orange juice for the dressing.

3. Prepare the dressing. Whisk the shallot together with the lime juice, lemon juice, grapefruit juice, orange juice, some salt and pepper and the olive oil.

4. Once the rice is cooked, run it under the cold tap until it has cooled. Drain away as much excess water as possible. Stir in the dressing, citrus pieces, seafood and watercress. Taste to see if it needs any more salt and pepper, and then serve straight away.

STORECUPBOARD

75g brown rice

freshly ground sea salt and black pepper

1 teaspoon extra virgin olive oil

FRESH

½ ruby grapefruit

1 orange

½ banana shallot, finely chopped

2 teaspoons lime juice

1 teaspoon lemon juice

2 handfuls of frozen mixed seafood, defrosted

2 large handfuls of watercress

ISRAELI CHOPPED MIXED BEAN SALAD

SERVES: 1 | **PREP TIME:** 10 minutes

A tin of mixed beans is a great starting point for any salad, but I like to combine it with a classic Israeli salad for a quick and crunchy bowlful at lunchtime. I say classic Israeli salad here because it includes tomatoes, cucumber, onion and lots of fresh parsley, all of which are essential components. However, you'll find that traditional recipes vary a lot.

I only use large tomatoes in the summer when they are nice and ripe; in the cooler months, you get a better flavour from cherry tomatoes.

1. Drain the beans and rinse off any extra liquid under the cold tap. Drain well and transfer to a mixing bowl.

2. Chop the cucumber, spring onion and the tomatoes into equal pieces, about the same size as the beans. Stir all of the chopped salad items and parsley into the beans. Add the oil, lemon juice and a generous few grinds of salt and pepper to the salad, and stir until everything is combined. Taste to see if you want to add any more lemon juice for tartness, salt if it is still a bit too bland, or pepper for flavour.

3. Transfer to a bowl, and sprinkle with the za'atar just before eating.

STORECUPBOARD

1 teaspoon extra virgin olive oil

freshly ground sea salt and black pepper

FRESH

1 x 400g tin mixed beans, drained

¼ cucumber

1 large spring onion, trimmed

a large handful of cherry tomatoes or 2 large tomatoes

a large handful of fresh flat-leaf parsley, roughly chopped

1 teaspoon lemon juice

½ teaspoon za'atar

BLTA CHOPPED SALAD WITH SKINNY BUTTERMILK RANCH DRESSING

SERVES: 1 | **PREP TIME:** 10 minutes | **COOKING TIME:** 5 minutes

I love a good, American-style chopped salad where all the pieces (including the lettuce) are cut up into same size pieces before being tossed in the salad dressing. This is a classic BLT (with added avocado) in salad form. Let it win you over to the world of chopped salads forever.

1. Fry the bacon in a (preferably non-stick) frying pan over a high heat, without any extra cooking fat, until the bacon is crispy.

2. Using a pair of scissors, snip the bacon into small pieces and toss all of the ingredients together with about 1 tablespoon of the dressing until everything is just coated. Eat immediately.

FRESH

2 rashers of streaky bacon

1 Little Gem lettuce, sliced

1 small ripe avocado, cut into chunks

1 spring onion, trimmed and chopped

a large handful of cherry tomatoes, quartered

Skinny Buttermilk Ranch Dressing (page 67)

HOT SALMON & AVOCADO SALAD WITH SOURED CREAM & LIME DRESSING

SERVES: 2 | **PREP TIME**: 10 minutes | **COOKING TIME**: 15–20 minutes

While it's fairly standard to use different textures and flavours in a salad to make life a bit more interesting, mixing hot and cold ingredients is more unusual. This is what I love about this salad: a mixture of a cool creamy dressing, room-temperature avocado and hot poached salmon.

1. Preheat the oven to 200°C/400°F/Gas mark 6.

2. Lay the salmon on a piece of tin foil and gather the sides up slightly to create a boat-like shape. Splash some white wine or water over the salmon, and season well with salt and pepper. Fold the top of the foil over so the package is sealed, but there is space inside for the salmon to steam. Place on a baking tray and bake for 15 to 20 minutes, until the salmon is flaky, but still slightly pink in the middle.

3. Meanwhile, prepare the rest of the salad. Arrange the salad leaves in two bowls. Divide the avocado, spring onion and sugar snaps between the bowls, and sprinkle over the sunflower seeds.

4. Drain away the cooking liquid from the salmon, and remove the skin. Using a fork, flake the salmon and divide it between the two salad portions. Drizzle over a generous amount of dressing, and eat immediately.

STORECUPBOARD

freshly ground sea salt and black pepper

FRESH

1 salmon fillet

a splash of white wine or water

4–5 large handfuls of salad leaves

1 large ripe avocado, chopped

2 large spring onions, trimmed and chopped

2 small handfuls of sugar snap peas, sliced

a handful of sunflower seeds

Soured Cream & Lime Dressing (page 69)

LEFTOVER ROAST CHICKEN, PESTO MAYO & TOMATO SANDWICH

SERVES: 1 | PREP TIME: 5 minutes

If you don't have enough chicken leftover to make a pie (page 140) after you've made my Easy Lemon & Thyme Roast Chicken (page 138), make a chicken sandwich instead. Wrapped in tin foil and packed up for later, this is a real treat.

1. Combine the mayonnaise and pesto and add the chicken. Stir until the chicken is well coated. Pile the chicken mayonnaise on to a slice of bread and season with salt and pepper. Spread the tomato over the top and add the second bread slice.

STORECUPBOARD

2 tablespoons light mayonnaise

½ teaspoon pesto

freshly ground sea salt and black pepper

FRESH

a large handful of shredded leftover Easy Lemon & Thyme Roast Chicken (page 138)

1 large tomato, thinly sliced

2 slices of bread

TIP: If you want to use sliced bread from the freezer, let it defrost on a plate covered in cling film. This will make the bread as soft as it was before you froze it.

WELSH RAREBIT

SERVES 1 | **PREP TIME**: 5 minutes | **COOKING TIME**: 5 minutes

This is my mother's variation on the classic Welsh rarebit. She usually makes it for my dad at lunchtime, changed up a little from how my grandmother used to make it for my grandfather.

My mother's recipe uses English mustard powder, and while it is better here, you can also sub it out for a teaspoon of Dijon mustard if you don't have any.

1. Preheat the grill as high as it will go and toast the bread in the toaster. Meanwhile, mash together the cheese, Worcestershire sauce, mustard powder, milk and a generous amount of salt and pepper to make a chunky paste. Depending on what type of cheese you're using, you may need to add a splash more milk.

2. Spread the cheese mixture over the toast, making sure you spread it right to the very edges. If you don't, any exposed bits will burn. Grill until the cheese is golden and bubbling; this can take anything from 1 to 5 minutes, again depending on the type of cheese you're using.

STORECUPBOARD

4 shakes of Worcestershire sauce

freshly ground sea salt and black pepper

FRESH

2 slices of bread

2 handfuls of grated hard cheese (approximately 70g)

½ teaspoon English mustard powder

½ tablespoon milk

DEVILLED EGG SANDWICH

SERVES: 1 | **PREP TIME:** 10 minutes | **COOKING TIME:** 10 minutes

An egg salad sandwich is a classic, but I bet you've never thought of making a devilled egg sandwich before, have you? These two retro egg dishes combined make a delicious sandwich with a bit of a kick from the mustard and Tabasco. If you're a cress person, feel free to add some, too.

1. Boil the eggs in a pan of boiling water set over a high heat for 10 minutes.

2. Run the eggs under cold water to cool them enough so that you can easily peel them. Once you've removed the shells, chop the eggs. Combine the chopped egg with the spring onion, parsley, mayonnaise, mustard, some salt and pepper and a good splash of Tabasco. Add a little bit more if you like things spicy.

3. Spread the egg mixture right to the edges of a slice of bread. Top with the salad and second slice of bread.

STORECUPBOARD

2 tablespoons light mayonnaise

¼ teaspoon Dijon mustard

freshly ground sea salt and black pepper

a splash of Tabasco

FRESH

2 large eggs

1 small spring onion, trimmed and finely chopped

a small handful of fresh parsley, finely chopped

a small handful of salad leaves

2 slices of bread

MACKEREL MAYO & QUICK-PICKLED CUCUMBER SANDWICHES

SERVES: 2 | **PREP TIME:** 10 minutes

I came up with this sandwich because I got bored of plain old tuna mayo. I like how the quick-pickled cucumber ribbons make this sandwich rather unique. Toasting the bread is a personal preference; I think the flavour works better with the smoked fish, but it's up to you.

1. In a small bowl, whisk together the vinegar, sugar and ½ teaspoon sea salt. Using a vegetable peeler or a very sharp knife, cut the cucumber into very thin ribbons – you don't need to bother peeling it. Add the cucumber ribbons to the bowl, and mix so that the cucumber is well coated in the pickling liquid. Set aside to pickle while you're making the rest of the sandwich filling.

2. Drain the mackerel and combine with the yoghurt. Season to taste with salt and pepper and lemon juice.

3. Toast the bread. While the bread is toasting, squeeze any excess liquid out of the cucumber ribbons.

4. To assemble the sandwich, divide the mackerel between two pieces of toast and spread it out to the corners. Lay the cucumber ribbons over the fish and grind over some pepper. Top with the toast slices and cut the sandwiches into rounds before serving.

STORECUPBOARD

1 tablespoon white wine vinegar

1 teaspoon golden caster sugar

freshly ground sea salt and black pepper

FRESH

¼ cucumber

1 x 110g tin smoked mackerel

2 tablespoons Greek yoghurt

a squeeze of lemon juice

4 slices of bread

SUPER VEGGIE RAINBOW WRAPS

SERVES: 2 | **PREP TIME:** 15 minutes

I love a good salad wrap at lunchtime, made with whatever I can find in the fridge. Wraps just feel much fancier than sandwiches. A rainbow selection of peppers, cucumber, carrot, red cabbage and spring onions, all held together with a generous scraping of mayonnaise, is a fantastic combination.

1. Slice the carrot, pepper, cucumber and spring onions into the thinnest matchsticks you can manage and shred the cabbage.

2. Divide the mayonnaise between the tortillas and spread it out evenly. Season the mayonnaise well with salt and pepper. Divide the vegetables between the tortillas and wrap up ready to enjoy.

STORECUPBOARD

1 tablespoon light mayonnaise

freshly ground sea salt and black pepper

FRESH

1 small carrot, peeled

½ red pepper, deseeded

a large chunk of cucumber

2 spring onions, trimmed

⅛ red cabbage

2 large tortilla wraps

BACON & AVOCADO WRAPS WITH SKINNY BUTTERMILK RANCH DRESSING

SERVES: 2 | **PREP TIME:** 5 minutes | **COOKING TIME:** 5 minutes

Bacon and avocado are a winning combination, especially when they are smothered in my lighter version of the all-American classic buttermilk ranch dressing. The quantities here will make more dressing than you need for this recipe; it will keep in the fridge in a sealed jam jar for 2 to 3 days and it is integral to my BLTA Chopped Salad (page 60).

I. To make the dressing, combine the mayonnaise, yoghurt and buttermilk until smooth. If you would like the dressing a little runnier, add a little cold water. To crush the garlic pieces, sprinkle over the salt and scrape over the garlic with a large, sharp knife at an angle. Stir the crushed garlic and salt, along with the chives (if you're using them), into the dressing. Taste, and add a little more salt if you think it needs it.

2. Fry the bacon in a large (preferably non-stick) frying pan over a high heat, without any additional fat, until it is cooked through and slightly crispy around the edges (I like to cut the bacon into bite-sized pieces using a pair of scissors, but you don't have to).

3. Assemble the wraps by dividing the bacon, avocado and lettuce or salad leaves between the tortillas. Drizzle over the dressing, then roll up and enjoy straight away while the bacon is still warm.

STORECUPBOARD

2 tablespoons light mayonnaise

I very small garlic clove, chopped

a large pinch of sea salt

FRESH

I tablespoon light Greek yoghurt

2½ tablespoons buttermilk

2 teaspoons finely snipped fresh chives (optional)

4 rashers of streaky bacon

I large ripe avocado, chopped

I Little Gem lettuce, shredded, or mixed salad leaves

2 large tortilla wraps

PILCHARDS ON TOAST

SERVES: 1 | **PREP TIME:** 5 minutes | **COOKING TIME:** 5 minutes

This is something my father likes to eat for lunch. Every time he makes it, I get treated to a lecture on how this was the type of 'simple' food they used to eat in the seventies. All I know is that it is cheap, easy and bloody delicious.

On the other hand, if you're after a quick 'something on toast' that does not require turning on the grill, cream cheese, za'atar and a good drizzle of extra virgin olive oil is one of my all-time favourite combinations. Another great one is a large handful of defrosted frozen peas mashed up with some lemon zest, a lot of freshly ground salt and pepper and, again, a good drizzle of extra virgin. If you have any leftover fresh mozzarella or fresh mint, tear them up and throw them in as well.

1. Toast the bread and preheat the grill to 250°C/485°F.

2. Tip the pilchards and their sauce into a bowl and, using a fork, mash into a rough paste with a good few fishy chunks left in.

3. Divide the mashed pilchards between the two pieces of toast and, using the fork, spread the pilchards right to the edges of the toast. Season each piece with a bit of salt.

4. Grill for 5 minutes until the fish topping has started to crisp up at the edges.

STORECUPBOARD

freshly ground sea salt

FRESH

2 slices of bread
(preferably the ends)

1 x 155g tin pilchards
in tomato sauce

LOADED FAJITA SALAD WITH SOURED CREAM & LIME DRESSING

SERVES: 1 | **PREP TIME**: 10 minutes | **COOKING TIME**: 10 minutes

This bright, Tex-Mex-inspired salad is made with leftovers. The salad and the tortilla chips can be made ahead and the fajita filling is easily microwaved, which accounts for both the quick cooking and preparation time in this recipe, and makes it the perfect desk lunch.

If you have any leftover homemade Pico de Gallo Salsa (page 127), or you fancy making some Boozy Guacamole (page 127), they will also be delicious added to the mix. You can use black beans instead of the red kidney beans, if you prefer, or a mixture of both.

1. Preheat the oven to 200°C/400°F/Gas mark 6.

2. Using a pair of scissors, cut the tortilla into triangles and spread them out on a baking tray. Bake them in the oven for 5 minutes or so, until they are crisp and golden around the edges. This method is also great for making chips to go with salsa or guacamole.

3. Meanwhile, make the dressing by combining the soured cream and lime juice, and season to taste with sea salt. Arrange the salad leaves and the kidney beans in a bowl and microwave the fajita chicken and peppers until heated through.

4. To serve, arrange the tortilla chips and the fajita filling at the side of the bowl, and spoon the dressing all over. If you have any fresh coriander or lime wedges in the fridge, serve the salad with these. However, they're not essential to a delicious bowlful.

STORECUPBOARD

freshly ground sea salt

FRESH

1 flour tortilla

3 tablespoons soured cream

juice of ¼ lime

2 large handfuls of salad leaves

250g tinned red kidney beans (drained weight)

1 portion of chicken and peppers from the Chicken Fajitas (page 126)

CAJUN PRAWN TACOS

MAKES: 6 tacos | **PREP TIME:** 10 minutes | **COOKING TIME:** 3 minutes

Tacos are always a good idea. You can fill them with pretty much anything that could be described as Mexican in flavour, but my favourite tacos are made with my super-easy, super-delicious Cajun prawns. The prawns are also great in salads, skewered and barbecued, or served on cocktail sticks by way of an easy summer canapé with a **Classic Margarita** (page 174) **or two.**

1. Combine the lime juice, oil and Cajun spice mix in a small bowl and add the prawns, tossing until well coated. Set aside to marinate while you prepare the rest of the taco accompaniments.

2. Leave the red onion to soak in a bowl of cold water, then drain and pat dry with kitchen paper (soaking the onion will remove some of the bite from the raw onion). Place the onion, coriander, soured cream and lime dressing and the guacamole in small bowls.

3. Heat a small (preferably non-stick) frying pan over a medium-high heat. Once the pan is hot, tip in the prawns and all of their marinade. Cook the prawns, stirring every 30 seconds or so, for about 3 minutes, until the prawns are just cooked through (they've gone from translucent and blue to pink and solid) and the marinade has formed a thick sauce. Transfer to a warm bowl and carry everything to the table with the warm tortillas for everyone to assemble the tacos themselves.

STORECUPBOARD

½ tablespoon light oil

¼ red onion, thinly sliced

FRESH

juice of ½ lime

1 tablespoon Cajun spice mix

18 raw prawns

a large handful of fresh coriander, leaves picked

Soured Cream & Lime Dressing (page 69)

Boozy Guacamole (page 127)

6 taco-size tortillas

LEFTOVER FAJITA BURRITOS

SERVES: 2 | **PREP TIME:** 5 minutes | **COOKING TIME:** 35 minutes

If you're serving fajitas up for a crowd (page 126), chances are that you may have a bit of meat, veg, and not to mention accompaniments like salsa and soured cream, left over. These burritos are the reason I make extra on purpose so that I'm guaranteed to have a bit left to play with.

Once you've made up the basic rice mixture, you can use anything, including grated cheese, leftover guacamole, soured cream, salsa and black beans, to build your burritos.

1. Cook the rice in a saucepan full of boiling water for 25 minutes. I cook rice like pasta and drain it once it is cooked. I promise you if you use this method rather than measuring out water and letting the rice absorb it all as it cooks, you'll never, ever have burnt, crunchy or dried out-rice.

2. Drain the rice and heat a splash of oil in a medium frying pan over a medium heat. Gently fry the onion for a few minutes until it has started to soften. Stir in the rice, cumin and a generous seasoning of sea salt.

3. Add the fajita chicken and peppers and the fresh coriander. Gently fry until the meat and vegetables are heated through. Squeeze over the lime juice and check you've added enough salt. Remove the pan from the heat.

4. Lay the tortillas on top of a double layer of foil. Divide the rice mixture between them. Add any additional burrito accompaniments and tightly roll up the wraps. Wrap around the foil to make them easy to hold, and eat immediately.

STORECUPBOARD

80g brown rice

a splash of light oil

½ red onion, finely chopped

½ teaspoon ground cumin

freshly ground sea salt

FRESH

1 portion of Chicken Fajitas (page 126)

a small handful of fresh coriander, finely chopped

juice of ¼ lime

2 flour tortillas

leftover Chicken Fajitas accompaniments (page 127)

LEFTOVER BREAD PANZANELLA

SERVES: 1 | **PREP TIME**: 10 minutes | **COOKING TIME**: 5 minutes

When you're living off a student budget, you come to hate wasting any scraps of food that you could otherwise turn into another dish. This salad is great in the summer when tomatoes are at their reddest and juiciest, and uses up the end of yesterday's loaf of bread.

I. Turn the grill up as high as it will go. Tear your leftover bread into ragged chunks that are small enough to eat in a single bite, and spread them out across a baking tray. Drizzle with I teaspoon of the oil, and season well with freshly ground salt and pepper. Put the tray under the grill, and toast the bread until it is just browned.

2. Meanwhile, leave the red onion in a dish of cold water. This will help take some of the bite out of it, making it much nicer to eat raw.

3. Transfer the toasted bread to a shallow bowl and throw in the basil, tomatoes, onion (patted dry on a piece of kitchen paper first) and capers. Toss so the tomato juices start to coat the bread, and drizzle over the remaining teaspoon of oil and the red wine vinegar. Toss again, season with a bit more freshly ground salt and pepper, and leave the bread to marinate for 10 minutes before tucking in.

STORECUPBOARD

2 teaspoons extra virgin olive oil

freshly ground sea salt and black pepper

½ red onion, thinly sliced

I tablespoon nonpareille capers

½ tablespoon red wine vinegar

FRESH

leftover stale bread

a small handful of fresh basil, torn

a generous handful of cherry tomatoes, halved or quartered

SLIGHTLY STICKY & SLIGHTLY SPICY CHICKEN WINGS

MAKES: 12 wings | **PREP TIME:** 10 minutes, plus 3 hours marinating | **COOKING TIME:** 30–40 minutes

I love chicken wings as you get a lot of bang for your buck: a better marinade-to-meat ratio than chicken drumsticks, and they're much easier to prepare than pork ribs. However, this slightly Asian marinade would be equally delicious with either of these, too.

1. Combine the soy sauce, Sriracha, sesame oil, honey, chopped garlic and a lot of freshly ground black pepper to create a smooth marinade. Transfer the chicken wings and the marinade to a large plastic bag. Tie a knot in the top of the bag, having pushed out as much air as possible. Mix the chicken wings around until they are well coated in the marinade. Refrigerate for at least 3 hours, but preferably overnight.

2. Take the wings out of the fridge to come up to room temperature while you preheat the oven to 180°C/350°F/Gas mark 4. Once the oven is hot, lay the wings out in a grill pan (you can take the grill pan out of the grill and use it in the oven). Bake for 30 to 40 minutes, basting the wings every 10 minutes or so with the leftover marinade from the bag and turning the wings over halfway through cooking. You can tell the wings are cooked through if the meat comes away easily when pulled with a fork. The marinade should create a sticky glaze.

STORECUPBOARD

4 tablespoons dark soy sauce

2 tablespoons runny honey

2 large garlic cloves, finely chopped

freshly ground black pepper

FRESH

8 teaspoons Sriracha

2 teaspoons toasted sesame oil

12 chicken wings

FATTOUSH

SERVES: 2 | **PREP TIME:** 15 minutes | **COOKING TIME:** 10 minutes

This punchy Middle Eastern salad is my favourite way to use up leftover stale pitta. This is the only recipe in the book that uses sumac, so if you don't have any other uses for it and you don't want to invest in a jar, za'atar makes a perfectly acceptable substitute here.

1. Place the onion slices in a small bowl with some cold water. Soaking will remove some of the bite from the raw onion.

2. Whisk together ½ tablespoon of the oil, the lemon juice and ½ teaspoon of the sumac to make the dressing. Set that aside, too.

3. Cut the cucumber, radishes and tomatoes into equal chunks and place in a bowl. You don't need to peel the cucumber.

4. Heat the rest of the oil in a large frying pan over a high heat. Tear the pittas into bite-sized chunks and fry them in the oil for about 10 minutes until they've started to crisp, tossing the pan as they fry. Season well with salt and pepper, and sprinkle over the rest of the sumac.

5. Drain the onion and dry on a piece of kitchen paper. Add to the salad. Toss the hot pitta pieces, the salad and the dressing together before serving immediately.

STORECUPBOARD

½ red onion, thinly sliced

3½ tablespoons extra virgin olive oil

freshly ground sea salt and black pepper

FRESH

juice of ½ lemon

1 teaspoon sumac

¼ cucumber

6 radishes

2 handfuls of cherry tomatoes

3 large pittas

1 Little Gem lettuce, shredded

a large handful of roughly chopped fresh parsley

INDIAN SPICED LEFTOVER SUMMER VEGETABLE FRITTERS

SERVES: 1 | **PREP TIME:** 10 minutes | **COOKING TIME:** 20 minutes

This recipe is designed to use up whatever summer vegetables or vegetable pieces you happen to have kicking around at the back of your fridge. The quantities suggested below are just a guide. These are great as part of a brunch spread or as a light summer meal with a green side salad.

1. Coarsely grate the potato, without peeling it, and then do the same with the courgette. Combine with the sea salt in a small bowl and set aside.

2. Beat together the egg, flour, baking powder, cumin and chilli powder in another bowl with a generous few grinds of black pepper to form a thick paste. Add the onion and the red pepper to the batter.

3. Over the sink, squeeze out any excess water from the potato and courgette mixture in handfuls, and add the grated vegetables to the batter. Stir until all of the vegetables are well coated.

4. Heat a very generous glug of oil in a (preferably non-stick) frying pan over a medium-high heat. Once the oil is hot and shimmering, fry about two spoonfuls of the batter-coated vegetables at a time for a few minutes on each side, until golden. Fry in batches, leaving the cooked fritters to drain on a couple of pieces of kitchen paper on a heated plate while you fry the rest.

5. Serve in a stack, sprinkled with fresh coriander.

STORECUPBOARD

½ teaspoon sea salt

3 tablespoons plain flour

½ teaspoon baking powder

1 teaspoon ground cumin

½ teaspoon chilli powder

freshly ground black pepper

¼ red onion, thinly sliced

light oil

FRESH

1 very small baking potato

½ courgette

1 large egg

¼ red pepper, deseeded and thinly sliced

fresh coriander, roughly chopped

LIGHT TZATZIKI WITH HOME-BAKED PITTA CHIPS

SERVES: 4–6 | PREP TIME: 15 minutes | COOKING TIME: 5 minutes

During the summer, you'll pretty much always find a big tub of homemade tzatziki in my fridge. It keeps for 3 to 4 days, and is great with my **Spiced Lamb Patties** (page 131), **Pork Souvlaki** (page 130), as part of a mezze or even as a salad dressing. I also love it with fresh toasted pitta (brushed with olive oil and sprinkled with dried oregano), or with home-baked pitta chips.

1. Preheat the oven to 200°C/400°F/Gas mark 6.

2. Coarsely grate the cucumber and set aside. To crush the garlic pieces, sprinkle over some sea salt and scrape over the garlic with a large, sharp knife at an angle. Combine the garlic and the dill in a large bowl with the yoghurt.

3. Over the kitchen sink, squeeze any excess liquid out of the grated cucumber and add to the yoghurt. Stir in the cucumber until everything is combined, and season to taste with lemon juice and sea salt. Set aside for the flavours to meld together while you're making the pitta chips.

4. Tear or cut (I like to use scissors for this) the pitta into manageable pieces. Spread them out across a baking tray and bake in the hot oven for 4 to 5 minutes until the pitta pieces are crisp and starting to go golden.

STORECUPBOARD

1 garlic clove, chopped

freshly ground sea salt

FRESH

1 cucumber

a small handful of fresh dill, finely chopped

1 x 500g tub light Greek yoghurt

a squeeze of lemon juice

6 pittas

PESTO, RICOTTA & PARMA HAM BAGEL PIZZAS

SERVES: 1 | **PREP TIME**: 5 minutes | **COOKING TIME**: 10 minutes

Bagel pizzas are one of my favourite 'I've got time to make it home but not to make anything fancy' lunches. They're also great for using up leftovers. Pesto, ricotta and Parma ham is one of my favourite combinations, but you can make a classic Italian version with any leftover tinned chopped tomatoes, passata or tomato purée you may have, plus a good handful of grated cheese melted on top and a few chopped olives.

1. Halve the bagel and spread each half with ricotta. Dot a few small dollops of pesto on top and drape over the pieces of ham. Season with salt and pepper, and grill until the ricotta is starting to go golden around the edges and the ham is beginning to crisp up.

STORECUPBOARD

pesto

freshly ground sea salt and black pepper

FRESH

1 bagel

2 tablespoons fresh ricotta

4 slices of Parma ham, prosciutto or wafer-thin ham

SOUPED-UP SAUSAGE ROLLS

MAKES: 4 large sausage rolls | **PREP TIME**: 15 minutes | **COOKING TIME**: 25 minutes

Using shop-bought puff pastry sheets and pre-seasoned sausage meat, these 'homemade' sausage rolls are child's play. However, you can take them to a whole other level by adding a few fresh herbs, some chopped ham and additional seasonings.

1. Preheat the oven to 200°C/400°F/Gas mark 6.

2. Take the ham and the parsley, along with the Worcestershire sauce, Tabasco and a generous amount of freshly ground salt and pepper, knead them into the sausage meat. The ham, sauces and parsley should be evenly distributed throughout the meat.

3. Quarter the pastry sheet with a sharp knife. Divide the sausage meat into four even portions and roll each into a sausage shape a couple of centimetres shorter than the length of each pastry piece. Position the sausage meat along the bottom of each pastry sheet, leaving just over 5mm at the bottom and along each side for sealing the roll.

4. Whisk the egg with a splash of cold water to make an egg wash, and paint this along the bottom edge and sides of each pastry sheet. Fold the sheets over to seal the sausage rolls. Be sure that each roll is well sealed, as any gaps will allow cooking juices from the sausage to leak out and give your sausage rolls a soggy bottom. Use a fork to make pretty lines around the edges of the rolls. Transfer to a baking sheet lined with baking parchment, and brush the exposed pastry with egg wash. Bake for 25 minutes until the pastry is crisp and golden.

STORECUPBOARD

½ teaspoon Worcestershire sauce

¼ teaspoon Tabasco

freshly ground sea salt and black pepper

FRESH

100g ham, roughly chopped

a small handful of fresh flat-leaf parsley, roughly chopped

350g sausage meat

1 x 320g all-butter puff pastry sheet

1 small egg

EASY SMOKED MACKEREL PÂTÉ

SERVES: 2 | **PREP TIME:** 5–10 minutes

If you always have a tin of smoked mackerel in the cupboard and a pot of yoghurt in the fridge, you'll be able to make up a delicious mackerel pâté for lunch. I like mine flavoured with fresh lemon, black pepper and chopped capers, but feel free to play around. Make it your own with your favourite flavours, or whatever you have to hand. If you have any fresh dill, chives or parsley, they are great here.

1. Drain the mackerel and mash it with a fork in a small bowl. Mix in the yoghurt. Stir the capers into the pâté. Season to taste with the lemon juice, sea salt and lots of black pepper. Serve with warm toast.

STORECUPBOARD

1 teaspoon nonpareille capers, chopped

freshly ground sea salt and black pepper

FRESH

1 x 110g tin smoked mackerel

3 tablespoons light Greek yoghurt

a squeeze of lemon juice

toast, to serve

ROAST BONE MARROW WITH GREMOLATA

SERVES: 1 | **PREP TIME:** 5 minutes | **COOKING TIME:** 10–15 minutes

Bone marrow may seem like a fancy restaurant ingredient, and not something you'd cook with at home. However, it is super-cheap and easy to cook, and is perfect served with something fresh and punchy on the side, like a classic gremolata.

1. Preheat the oven to 200°C/400°F/ Gas mark 6.

2. Place the bone cut side up on a baking tray and season well with salt and pepper. Roast for 10 to 15 minutes until the marrow becomes translucent.

3. Meanwhile, combine the garlic and parsley with the lemon zest and a generous pinch of sea salt.

4. Toast the bread and serve alongside the roasted marrow and gremolata.

STORECUPBOARD

freshly ground sea salt and black pepper

1 large garlic clove, finely chopped

FRESH

1 piece of bone marrow, halved lengthways

a small handful of fresh flat-leaf parsley, chopped

zest of ½ lemon

2 thick slices of bread, to serve

INDIAN SPICED POTATOES

SERVES: 1 | **PREP TIME**: 5 minutes | **COOKING TIME**: 15 minutes

While my version of Indian Spiced Potatoes make a great side dish (multiply these quantities by the amount of people you want to feed), I also like to eat a bowlful by themselves as a quick meal. Pile on some yoghurt and fresh coriander, and even some mango chutney if you have any, to enhance the dish.

1. Cube the baking potato (don't worry about peeling it) and place in a saucepan with a pinch of salt and enough cold water to just cover the potatoes. Set over a very high heat with a lid on and bring to the boil. Cook the potato pieces for 10 minutes until just tender. Remove from the heat and drain.

2. Heat the oil in a medium or large frying pan over a high heat. Once the oil is just smoking, add the potato and the spices. Toss everything well until the potato pieces are well coated. Fry for about 5 minutes, tossing the potato around the pan every minute or so, until crispy. Finish with a squeeze of lemon juice.

STORECUPBOARD

sea salt

1 tablespoon light oil

¼ teaspoon ground cumin

¼ teaspoon chilli powder

FRESH

1 large baking potato

¼ teaspoon ground tumeric

a large pinch of ground coriander

a squeeze of lemon juice

MUSHROOMS ON TOAST WITH TAMAGO RIBBONS

SERVES: 2 | **PREP TIME:** 5 minutes | **COOKING TIME:** 10 minutes

STORECUPBOARD

freshly ground black pepper

1 teaspoon dark soy sauce

FRESH

a large and a small knob of unsalted butter

4 thick slices of bread

6–8 shiitake mushrooms, thickly sliced

1 large egg

1 teaspoon mirin

a small handful of fresh coriander, roughly chopped

Sometimes the best dishes come out of whatever is left over in your fridge. I like to use shiitake mushrooms here (you can now find them fresh in most supermarkets) to fit in with the idea that this is essentially Asian mushrooms and egg on toast, but chestnut mushrooms will do. Tamago is a type of Japanese omelette that I think makes the most delicious garnish.

1. In a large frying pan, heat the large knob of butter over a medium heat until frothy. Toast the bread and leave it in the toaster so that it stays warm.

2. Gently fry the mushrooms in the butter until they are soft and starting to brown. Season well with black pepper and stir in the soy sauce. Don't season with any salt, as there is enough salt in the soy sauce already.

3. Leave the mushrooms in the pan over the lowest heat you can to keep warm while you cook the egg. If you're good at kitchen management, it is possible to cook the egg and the mushrooms simultaneously, but it is not a requirement!

4. Whisk the egg together with the mirin. Heat the smaller butter knob in a small frying pan over a medium heat, and when it is frothy pour in the egg mixture to cover the base of the pan. Let it cook until it is just set, then slide it out of the pan onto a chopping board. Roll up the cooked egg and cut it into ribbons.

5. Spoon the mushrooms over the toast and top with the tamago ribbons. Sprinkle with the chopped herbs and finish with a good few grinds of black pepper.

TEN-MINUTE MUSHROOMS & BACON ON TOAST

SERVES: 1 | **PREP TIME**: 5 minutes | **COOKING TIME**: 5 minutes

STORECUPBOARD

freshly ground sea salt and black pepper

FRESH

2 rashers of streaky bacon

a large knob of unsalted butter

2 slices of bread

6 chestnut mushrooms, sliced

2 large spring onions, trimmed and sliced

Mushrooms on toast are usually something I can throw together from the fridge for a quick and satisfying breakfast, lunch or dinner. Alternatively, forget the bacon and add a spoonful each of Dijon and wholegrain mustard and a good few dollops of either cream or crème fraîche (not yoghurt though, as it will split in the pan). Now you have a creamy, mustardy veggie version that is equally satisfying.

1. Chop the bacon (I find it easiest to use a pair of scissors). Heat the butter in a medium frying pan set over a medium-high heat. Toast the bread, and leave it in the toaster to stay warm.

2. Once the butter is frothy, add the mushrooms, bacon and spring onion and fry until the mushrooms are soft and the bacon is starting to turn golden. Season well with salt and pepper, and spoon over the hot toast. I don't butter my toast, but you may like to.

SOLO DINNERS

PASTA 88

SOUPS 96

WEEKNIGHT WONDERS 99

BETTER THAN TAKEAWAY 110

GRATED COURGETTE PASTA

MAKES: 1 portion | **PREP TIME:** 5 minutes | **COOKING TIME:** 15 minutes

Forget pricey spiralizers. You want to grate your courgette and mix it with the pasta so many people are seeking to replace. Usually when I'm after a quick, light pasta supper, I don't even need the recipe to make this anymore. Just use a good-sized courgette, some fresh lemon, a good glug of extra virgin olive oil, a little bit of fresh or dried red chilli and lots of salt and pepper. You can also add some fresh torn basil in here, if you have some, but it's not essential for a delicious bowlful.

1. Put the pasta on to cook in a saucepan of salted boiling water over a high heat. Meanwhile, coarsely grate the courgette.

2. When the pasta is al dente (this should take about 10 to 12 minutes), drain and return it to the saucepan along with the rest of the ingredients and a generous amount of freshly ground salt and pepper. Return to the heat and stir until everything is combined and the courgette has coated the pasta. Serve in a warm bowl with a glass of cold white wine.

STORECUPBOARD

100g pasta shapes

1 teaspoon extra virgin olive oil

freshly ground sea salt and black pepper

FRESH

1 courgette

¼ fresh or dried red chilli, deseeded and thinly sliced, or a generous pinch of dried chilli flakes

zest of ½ lemon

juice of ¼ lemon

TINNED TOMATO PASTA SAUCE

MAKES: 2 portions | **PREP TIME**: 5 minutes | **COOKING TIME**: 10–15 minutes

This is the pasta sauce to make when you're in the market for a speedy pasta supper, but you haven't got any fresh ingredients in the house.

You can make this sauce into a steaming bowl of soup (to serve one) by making up half a vegetable stock cube in the empty tomato tin, adding it to the saucepan and simmering for 20 minutes instead of 10. Blend until smooth with a stick blender and whisk in 1 teaspoon crème fraîche or cream (whatever you happen to have in the fridge). The cream is optional, but really makes the soup taste like everyone's favourite tinned cream of tomato soup.

1. Heat a small saucepan over a medium heat. Add the butter. When the butter has melted and gone frothy, add the tomatoes, sugar and oregano to the saucepan. Season well with salt and pepper, and stir.

2. Leave the sauce bubbling away for 10 to 15 minutes, stirring occasionally, until it has thickened and is the consistency of a good pasta sauce.

STORECUPBOARD

1 x 400g tin chopped tomatoes

½ teaspoon dried oregano (or 1 teaspoon fresh oregano)

freshly ground sea salt and black pepper

FRESH

a small knob of unsalted butter

½ teaspoon soft light brown sugar

PASTA IN TOMATO, TUNA & CAPER SAUCE

MAKES: 1 portion | **PREP TIME:** 5 minutes | **COOKING TIME:** 15 minutes

Sometimes, all you want is pasta. This easy pasta sauce is packed with flavour, and is made out of things you are likely to have at the back of your kitchen cupboard.

1. Put the pasta on to cook in a saucepan of salted boiling water and cook over a high heat until al dente. This should take about 12 minutes. Meanwhile, make the sauce.

2. Add the garlic to a large frying pan, along with the capers and a generous glug of oil. Set over a medium heat and leave for a few minutes until the garlic and capers are sizzling, and the garlic has started to soften. Add the tomatoes to the pan and season well with salt and pepper. Reduce the heat to low, allowing the sauce to bubble away gently until the pasta is a few minutes away from being done.

3. Drain the tuna and add it to the tomato sauce, stirring it in until the fish is well coated in the sauce, but taking care not break up the tuna chunks too much.

4. Drain the pasta and stir it into the sauce. If you're using it, tear up the basil and stir it into the pasta. Taste a little of the sauce to check you're happy with the amount of salt and pepper, and serve.

STORECUPBOARD

100g pasta shapes

1 large garlic clove, finely chopped

1½ tablespoons nonpareille capers

light oil

1 x 250g tin chopped tomatoes

freshly ground sea salt and black pepper

FRESH

1 x 140g tin tuna in spring water or brine

a small handful of fresh basil (optional)

FROZEN SEAFOOD & WHITE WINE LINGUINI

MAKES: I portion | **PREP TIME:** 5 minutes | **COOKING TIME:** I5 minutes

Buying bags of mixed frozen seafood is actually pretty great value. Once defrosted they make a good substitute for fresh. If you use them from frozen, in a cooked dish like this, it is harder to overcook.

I've listed linguini here as I love the amount of bite in each strand, but spaghetti is fine, as well as tagliatelle or any other type of long pasta shape.

I. Cook the pasta in a saucepan of salted boiling water over a high heat until al dente. It should take about I2 minutes to cook.

2. Put the garlic, butter and a splash of oil in a large frying pan. Set it over a medium heat, and leave until the butter is melted and frothy, and the garlic has started to sizzle and soften. Add the lemon zest, white wine and a generous amount of salt and pepper. Stir, and add the seafood. Once the seafood has defrosted and has cooked for about 3 minutes (the prawns should be pink and firm), add the lemon juice and the parsley. Stir until everything is combined.

3. Drain the pasta and add it to the frying pan. Stir well until all of the strands are coated, and transfer to a warm bowl before tucking in.

STORECUPBOARD

I00g linguini

I large garlic clove, thinly sliced

light oil

freshly ground sea salt and black pepper

FRESH

a large knob of unsalted butter

zest of ½ lemon

30ml white wine

2 large handfuls of frozen mixed seafood

I tablespoon lemon juice

a small handful of fresh parsley, roughly chopped

BLISTERED CHERRY TOMATO PUTTANESCA

MAKES: 1 portion | **PREP TIME:** 5 minutes | **COOKING TIME:** 15 minutes

Puttanesca is another one of those storecupboard spaghetti classics. However, when you're cooking for just the one of you, it usually results in half a tin of tomatoes left over in the fridge. For an easy panful that won't yield any leftovers that need using up, cherry tomatoes are the answer. I also find that using fresh tomatoes makes the pasta fresher, brighter and full of sunshine.

1. Cook the spaghetti in a saucepan of generously salted boiling water over a high heat until al dente; this should take about for 12 minutes.

2. Set a large frying pan over a medium heat and add the garlic and the oil. A lot of recipes will tell you to heat the oil first and then add the garlic, but I have found that by adding the oil and the garlic together, and letting the oil heat up and the garlic gradually start to sizzle, the flavour of the garlic will infuse the oil better. It will also make it easier to prevent the garlic from burning.

3. When the garlic starts to sizzle, reduce the heat to medium low. Add the anchovies, capers and olives. Cook for about a minute until the anchovies have melted. Add the tomatoes and cook until soft and starting to fall apart, and their skins have blistered. Season generously with salt and pepper.

4. If you need to, remove the frying pan from the heat and set aside until the spaghetti is cooked. Once it is ready, return the frying pan to a low heat (if you're going straight in with the spaghetti, just turn the heat down to low) and add 2 tablespoons of the spaghetti cooking water to create a looser sauce. Drain the spaghetti and add to the frying pan. Stir the pasta into the sauce, still over the heat, until the strands are well coated. Stir in the basil, and serve straight away.

STORECUPBOARD

100g spaghetti

2 large garlic cloves, thinly sliced

2 teaspoons light oil

3 anchovy fillets in olive oil

2 teaspoons nonpareille capers

freshly ground sea salt and black pepper

FRESH

a small handful of pitted black olives, halved

150g (roughly 2 handfuls) cherry tomatoes, halved

a small handful of fresh basil, roughly chopped

ROASTED VEGETABLE PASTA

MAKES: 2 portions | **PREP TIME:** 10 minutes | **COOKING TIME:** 40 minutes

This is usually the first thing I make myself whenever I move into a new flat. Roasted Mediterranean vegetables are a wonderful thing to make in a big batch ready to enjoy later. Mix some of them with pasta, then pack up the rest (they are delicious cold) for lunch the next day. Aubergine would be good thrown in with these, too.

1. Preheat the oven to 200°C/400°F/Gas mark 6.

2. Cut all of the vegetables into manageable chunks. Toss the vegetables with the olive oil, either in a plastic bag or a large roasting tray, adding a generous amount of salt and pepper. If you're using the bag method, tip the vegetables into the roasting tray. Roast for 40 minutes, tossing halfway through.

3. After you've tossed the vegetables, put the pasta on to cook over a high heat in a large saucepan of salted boiling water for about 12 minutes. Once the pasta is ready, drain and return to the pan. Add the vegetables, and stir until the pasta is well coated in the roasting juices.

STORECUPBOARD

1 red onion

1 tablespoon extra virgin olive oil

freshly ground sea salt and black pepper

200g pasta shapes

FRESH

1 large courgette

2 red, yellow or orange peppers, deseeded

HAM, PESTO & MOZZARELLA PASTA BAKE

MAKES: 2 portions | **PREP TIME:** 10 minutes | **COOKING TIME:** 35–40 minutes

While this serves two, I always make it for myself as it is just as good, if not better, reheated. The inside remains soft and tender, and you get even more crispy, crunchy bits than just the breadcrumb topping.

I've made this with cheap ham here, and it is perfectly delicious. However, the better the ham you use, the better the pasta bake. You don't need exactly 100g, just whatever equivalent size pack you can find.

1. Cook the pasta in a large pan of salted boiling water over a high heat for 10 to 12 minutes, until the pasta is al dente. Preheat the grill to 200°C/400°F.

2. Drain the pasta, shaking off as much of the cooking water as possible. Add the pesto, ham and half of the mozzarella to the pan. Stir until everything is combined and evenly distributed. Transfer the pasta mixture to an ovenproof baking dish and scatter the top with the rest of the mozzarella. Sprinkle with breadcrumbs and season generously with freshly ground salt and pepper.

3. Grill the pasta bake for 15 to 20 minutes until the cheese is golden and bubbly, and the breadcrumbs are brown and crisp.

STORECUPBOARD

200g pasta shapes

4 tablespoons pesto

freshly ground sea salt and black pepper

FRESH

2 mozzarella balls, torn

1 x 100g pack wafer-thin ham, sliced into ribbons

4 tablespoons fresh breadcrumbs (see the notes on breadcrumbs, page 100)

FRYING-PAN LASAGNE

MAKES: 2 portions | **PREP TIME**: 5 minutes | **COOKING TIME**: 25 minutes

I love lasagne, but baking a dish of layered pasta, homemade white sauce, bolognese, cheese and sometimes tomatoes as well seems like far too much effort on a weeknight. You can make this lasagne in one frying pan, using leftovers, in less than half an hour. I've made this to serve two as this is as much as can possibly be fitted into a frying pan. However, halving the quantities to serve just you does not make it any easier to prepare, and this way you'll have a portion for another day.

I. Fill a medium frying pan with a heatproof handle two-thirds full with boiling water. Add a generous pinch of salt, the lasagne sheets, halved, and a splash of oil. Cook for about 12 to 15 minutes over a high heat (stirring occasionally to stop the pasta sticking to the bottom of the pan) until the pasta is al dente, and drain. While the pasta is cooking, tear the mozzarella into bite-sized pieces.

2. Preheat the grill to 250°C/485°F. Return the pasta to the pan along with the bolognese. Return to the heat, turned down to medium, and stir until everything is combined and the sauce is bubbling. Stir in half of the cheese until it starts to melt, then remove the pan from the heat.

3. Top with the rest of the cheese and a generous seasoning of salt and pepper. Put the pan under the grill for 4 to 5 minutes, until the cheese is starting to brown and bubble, and the exposed bits of pasta are beginning to go a little crispy.

STORECUPBOARD

light oil

freshly ground sea salt and black pepper

FRESH

6 dried lasagne sheets

2 portions of Sausage Bolognese (page 134)

2 mozzarella balls

CARROT SOUP

MAKES: 4–5 portions | **PREP TIME**: 15 minutes | **COOKING TIME**: 50–55 minutes

I'm a big soup maker and carrot has to be one of my favourites. I've made so many different versions of it, from basic, pared-down soups to spice-laced bowlfuls. This soup is also pretty cheap to make, especially when you buy bags of carrots at a reduced price when they're almost going soft. I've even found supermarket kilo bags as cheap as 27p before. This soup is also one of my favourite things to make in bulk, and then stash in single servings in the freezer.

1. Add the onion, garlic and oil to a large saucepan and set it over a medium heat. Fry until the onion and garlic are sizzling and starting to soften.

2. Add the carrots and cumin to the pan. Fry for about a minute.

3. Rinse the lentils in a sieve under a cold tap until the water runs clear, then stir them into the vegetables and spices.

4. Add the stock and bring to the boil, then reduce the heat to low. Leave the pan to simmer, uncovered, for 40 minutes. Season the soup with salt and pepper and blend until smooth with a stick blender.

5. Check if the soup needs any more seasoning before serving, topped with chopped fresh coriander, if you have any.

STORECUPBOARD

2 large onions, finely chopped

2 large garlic cloves, finely chopped

1 tablespoon light oil

2 teaspoons ground cumin

1.2 litres vegetable stock (made with 1 stock cube)

freshly ground sea salt and black pepper

FRESH

1kg carrots, peeled and cut into chunks

100g red split lentils

fresh coriander, roughly chopped (optional)

A BASIC CHICKEN SOUP

MAKES: 3–4 portions | **PREP TIME**: 10 minutes | **COOKING TIME**: 50 minutes

This basic, everyday chicken soup is great for using up the leftover scraps hanging around at the bottom of your fridge. Even better, it only takes an hour to make from start to finish. I wrote the recipe for this in my head during a class on classical epic poetry. I based it on what I could remember that I needed to use up at the time.

Serve with fresh crusty bread, and if you have any leftover fresh thyme hanging around, that would be great sprinkled on top of your bowl, too.

1. Add the garlic to a medium saucepan along with the chicken stock and the chicken breast. Bring the pan to the boil over a high heat. Once the water is bubbling, reduce the heat to medium-low and put a lid on the pan. Leave the pan to simmer for 20 minutes.

2. In a very large saucepan, heat the oil over a medium heat and gently fry the leek, celery and carrots until they are soft.

3 Remove the chicken breast from the saucepan and pour the simmering stock and garlic mixture into the vegetable pan. Using two forks, shred the chicken into manageable pieces and add them to the pan, too. Add the thyme and the brown rice. Season generously with salt and pepper, and leave to simmer with the lid on for 25 minutes.

4. Add the mushrooms to the pan. Allow to cook for another 5 minutes before serving.

STORECUPBOARD

1 large garlic clove, chopped

1 litre chicken stock (made with 1 stock cube)

1 tablespoon light oil

30g brown rice

freshly ground sea salt and black pepper

FRESH

1 large chicken breast

1 large leek, trimmed and sliced

2 celery sticks, finely chopped

2 large carrots, peeled and finely chopped

2 teaspoons dried or chopped fresh thyme

2 handfuls of mushrooms, sliced

QUICK & CREAMY PUMPKIN & COCONUT SOUP

MAKES: 2–3 portions | **PREP TIME**: 10 minutes | **COOKING TIME**: 25 minutes

This is another one of my favourite soups. It works best with a cooking pumpkin (though you can use kind sold for carving at Halloween) and you can also substitute with other types of squashes. However, bear in mind that some squashes such as butternut are sweeter than pumpkin, so you might want to leave out the honey and use it to sweeten the soup to taste later.

You can use any leftover coconut milk in my **Easy Root Vegetable Curry** (page 128) **or to make Coconut Hot Chocolate** (page 170).

1. Peel and remove the seeds from the pumpkin and cut the flesh into small cubes.

2. Add the garlic, onion and a good splash of oil to a medium saucepan. Set over a medium heat and cook until the garlic is sizzling and soft but not starting to brown. Add the stock cube and stir until it has broken down. Add the pumpkin and the honey to the pan, and season well with salt and pepper.

3. Pour enough boiling water into the saucepan to just cover the cubes of pumpkin, and leave to simmer with the lid on for 20 minutes.

4. Remove from the heat and blend until smooth with a stick blender. Blend in the coconut milk, and check you're happy with the seasoning. Serve each portion with a swirl of coconut milk and a generous sprinkling of fresh coriander, if you have any.

STORECUPBOARD

2 large garlic cloves, chopped

1 large onion, chopped

light oil

½ vegetable stock cube

1 tablespoon runny honey

freshly ground sea salt and black pepper

FRESH

600g pumpkin

3 tablespoons coconut milk, plus extra to serve

fresh coriander, roughly chopped (optional)

TUNA & PESTO RICE

MAKES: 1 portion | **PREP TIME**: 5 minutes | **COOKING TIME**: 25 minutes

I can't remember if it was my friend Steph or I who discovered that if you mix some pesto and a tin of tuna into a pouch of microwave rice (plain, brown or sun-dried tomato flavour) you have a super-quick, super-delicious meal that involves literally no effort at all. For something more substantial, a fried egg on top is always a good idea.

I've cooked rice from scratch here to make this bowlful because it is cheaper, but feel free to buy it pre-cooked in a pouch if you're looking for something super-speedy.

1. Cook the rice in a saucepan full of boiling water for 25 minutes. I cook rice like pasta and drain it once it is cooked. I promise you, if you use this method rather than measuring out water and letting the rice absorb it as it cooks, you'll never, ever have burnt, crunchy or dried-out rice.

2. Drain the tuna, and stir it into the rice, along with the pesto. Season to taste with salt and pepper.

STORECUPBOARD

100g brown rice

3 tablespoons pesto

freshly ground sea salt and black pepper

FRESH

1 x 200g tin tuna in spring water or brine

CRUNCHY PESTO-BAKED SALMON FILLETS WITH BLACKENED KALE

MAKES: I portion | **PREP TIME:** 5 minutes | **COOKING TIME:** I5 minutes

Salmon and pesto is a surprisingly amazing combination. This dish is equally good doubled as a date-night dish with fancy fresh bread and salad, or for a healthy weeknight with brown rice.

I. Preheat the oven to I80°C/350°F/Gas mark 4.

2. Place the salmon fillet skin side down on a baking tray lined with baking parchment.

3. Combine 3 tablespoons of the breadcrumbs and half the grated Parmesan with the pesto and a generous amount of salt and pepper.

4. Press the pesto breadcrumb mix onto the top of the fillet to form a crust. Top the crust with the rest of the cheese and breadcrumbs. Season with a little more salt and pepper and bake in the oven for I5 minutes.

5. While the salmon is baking, cook the kale. Remove any pieces of stem from the chopped kale, and heat a splash of oil in a large frying pan over a very high heat. Once the oil is smoking, add the kale and fry, tossing occasionally until the kale is tender and crisp in parts. Serve with the salmon straight away, with the lemon wedge for squeezing over.

Breadcrumbs: You can buy them in a packet (if you don't use them in one go you can keep them in the freezer; they should stay loose so you can defrost however much you want to use each time) or make your own. If you happen to have a mini chopper or a food processor you can make them out of whatever stale hunks of bread you have lying around. You can also keep these chunks in the freezer to make breadcrumbs when you need them. Breadcrumbs made with stale bread also keep a surprisingly long time in a clean, sealed jar in the fridge.

STORECUPBOARD

I½ tablespoons pesto

freshly ground sea salt and black pepper

light oil

FRESH

I salmon fillet

3½ tablespoons breadcrumbs

2 teaspoons freshly grated Parmesan cheese

2 very large handfuls of chopped kale

I lemon wedge, to serve

KITCHEN CUPBOARD FISHCAKES

MAKES: 5 fishcakes | **PREP TIME**: 20 minutes, plus 30 minutes chilling | **COOKING TIME**: 40 minutes

These fishcakes are great because they're made pretty much entirely out of the things you've usually got kicking around your kitchen cupboard. I love them with a good side salad for a solo supper, with a dollop of mayonnaise and some lemon wedges for squeezing over. Individually wrap them before freezing, and then you can cook them from frozen.

You can use dried breadcrumbs or shop-bought fresh. Matzo meal is my favourite here if your local supermarket stocks it in the kosher section. Polenta, however, is a bad idea. If you have any leftover parsley or dill in the bottom of the fridge, chop it up and add it to the mix, too.

1. Place the potato in a medium saucepan with a generous amount of salt and enough cold water to cover the potato. Set over a high heat and bring to the boil. Cook for 20 minutes until the potato is tender.

2. Meanwhile, drain the fish and break it up in a small bowl to form a rough paste but still with a few good chunks in it. Pour over the milk, and mix in.

3. Once the potato is cooked, drain away the water, and mash until smooth with the butter, mayonnaise and mustard. Add the fish and milk mixture, the spring onion, lemon zest and a generous amount of salt and pepper. Mix until everything is combined, and shape the mixture into five fishcakes. Leave these to chill and harden in the fridge for half an hour.

4. Preheat the oven to 220°C/425°F/Gas mark 7.

5. Crack the egg into a shallow bowl and whisk. Put the flour on a plate, and the breadcrumbs on another one. Dip the fishcakes first in the flour, then the egg, then the breadcrumbs. I tend to use one hand for coating the fishcakes in the egg and another for dipping them in the dry ingredients so that I'm not breadcrumbing my fingers!

6. Bake the fishcakes you're planning on eating right away on a baking tray for 20 minutes until the breadcrumbs are golden. Individually wrap the others in cling film before freezing.

STORECUPBOARD

1 tablespoon light mayonnaise

½ teaspoon Dijon mustard

freshly ground sea salt and black pepper

2 tablespoons plain flour

FRESH

1 very large potato, peeled and quartered

1 x 200g tin tuna in spring water or brine

1 x 110g tin smoked mackerel

1 tablespoon milk

a large knob of unsalted butter

2 large spring onions, trimmed and finely chopped

zest of ½ lemon

1 large egg

3 tablespoons breadcrumbs

LIGHTER TUNA & SWEETCORN BAKED SWEET POTATO

MAKES: 1 portion | **PREP TIME:** 5 minutes | **COOKING TIME:** 45 minutes

I promise you that after you've made tuna mayo with a mixture of mayonnaise and yoghurt, you'll never make it with just mayonnaise again. It is lighter, fresher and simply more delicious piled like this on top of a baked sweet potato.

If you're after any other baked sweet potato ideas, they're great topped with a couple of spoonfuls of reheated leftover **Super-Easy Meat-Free Mixed Bean Chilli** (page 132) **or a fresh batch of Boozy Guacamole** (page 127) **and whatever Pico de Gallo Salsa** (page 127) **you have left over from other dishes.**

1. Preheat the oven to 220°C/425°F/Gas mark 7.

2. Pierce the sweet potato all over with a sharp knife and bake in the oven for 45 minutes until tender.

3. Drain the tuna and mix it with the yoghurt, mayonnaise and a generous amount of freshly ground salt and pepper until everything is combined. Combine three-quarters of the spring onion with the sweetcorn and the tuna.

4. Once the sweet potato is cooked, slash the top and pile on the tuna mixture, followed by the remaining spring onion before serving.

STORECUPBOARD

1 tablespoon light mayonnaise

freshly ground sea salt and black pepper

FRESH

1 medium sweet potato

1 x 120g tin tuna in spring water or brine

4 tablespoons Greek yoghurt

1 large spring onion, trimmed and thinly sliced

a large handful of tinned sweetcorn

TWICE-COOKED PIZZA BAKED POTATO

MAKES: 1 portion | **PREP TIME:** 10 minutes | **COOKING TIME:** 1 hour 30 minutes

Baked potatoes are easy. You can run with so many different toppings, and bake a couple at once, ready to be reheated later. While baking the potatoes and the toppings separately is the easiest way to go, you can take your baked potato to a whole new level by baking it again with a cheesy topping.

Everything you'd usually put on a pizza works brilliantly. If you have any Sausage Bolognese (page 134) left over, it is great spooned over a split potato, topped with a handful of grated cheese and baked until golden and bubbling.

1. Preheat the oven to 200°C/400°F/ Gas mark 6.

2. Pierce the potato with a sharp knife, and wrap it in foil. Bake in the oven for 1¼ hours. (You'll only need 1 hour for a smaller potato.)

3. Remove the potato from the foil and slash the top in each direction. Place it on a baking tray and mash the potato in the middle a little. Top with the passata, your chosen pizza toppings and the cheese. Return to the oven for 15 minutes until the cheese is golden and bubbling.

FRESH

1 medium baking potato

4 tablespoons passata

your choice of pizza toppings (e.g. fresh basil, chorizo, ham, olives, etc.)

½ mozzarella ball, roughly torn

GAMMON & EGG WITH CAJUN POTATO WEDGES

MAKES: 1 portion │ **PREP TIME:** 15 minutes │ **COOKING TIME:** 40 minutes

This is my (Cajun-spiced) take on that English classic: ham, egg and chips. Cajun spice mix is one of my spice cupboard heroes. It is an essential ingredients for both my Cajun Prawn Tacos (page 70) and my Super-Easy Meat-Free Mixed Bean Chilli (page 132). Gammon steaks typically come in packs of two. Either double up if there are two of you eating, or freeze the other for later.

1. Preheat the oven to 200°C/400°F/Gas mark 6.

2. Cut the potatoes into wedges, and place in a saucepan with some salt and enough cold water to cover the potatoes. Set over a high heat, bring to the boil (a lid is handy, but not essential here) and parboil the potatoes for 10 minutes.

3. Remove the pan from the heat and drain the potatoes. Place them in a plastic bag with 1 tablespoon of the oil, the spice mix and a generous amount of freshly ground salt and pepper. Seal the bag and shake until the potatoes are well coated. Spread the potatoes out in a baking tray, lined with tin foil if you are a washing-up dodger like me. Bake them in the oven for 30 minutes, tossing them around on the tray halfway through.

4. Meanwhile, preheat the grill to 220°C/425°F. You'll want to grill the gammon about 10 minutes and fry your egg about 5 minutes before the potatoes are ready.

5. Now, different gammon steaks take different amounts of time to cook. Typically they should take 3 to 5 minutes on each side, and they should curl up a little at the edges like bacon when it is time to turn them over. They are ready to eat when they look like they're ready, again just like bacon.

6. Meanwhile, fry the egg in a small frying pan over a high heat, with just a splash of oil in the pan, and serve with the potato wedges and gammon.

STORECUPBOARD

light oil

freshly ground sea salt and black pepper

FRESH

2 medium potatoes

1 tablespoon Cajun spice mix

1 gammon steak

1 large egg

CHICKEN SCHNITZEL WITH CAPERS, ANCHOVIES & A FRIED EGG

MAKES: 1 portion | **PREP TIME:** 10 minutes | **COOKING TIME:** 15 minutes

Schnitzel, that great Austrian classic. I like mine with a massive hit of salty capers and anchovies on top, plus a fried egg that has a runny, golden-yellow yolk. You can use dried breadcrumbs or shop-bought fresh (see the note on page 100). Matzo meal is my favourite here if your local supermarket has a kosher section.

For a lighter option you can serve this with a green salad, but I like to keep it rooted firmly as a comfort food dish with a side of Mustard Mash (page 120).

1. Crack one of the eggs into a bowl and add the mustard along with some freshly ground salt and pepper. Beat together until smooth. Sprinkle the flour on a plate, and the breadcrumbs on another one.

2. Using a large sharp knife, slice the chicken breast horizontally, almost to the end, then open it out into one large, thin piece of chicken. Using the heel of your hand, bash this out until the chicken is as thin as you can get it without breaking it up.

3. Coat the chicken in flour, followed by the egg mixture, then the breadcrumbs. Use one hand for the dry ingredients and another for dipping the chicken in the egg to avoid breadcrumbing your fingers!

4. Heat a couple of centimetres of oil in a medium frying pan over a high heat until the oil is shimmering. Fry the chicken for 7 to 8 minutes on each side until the breadcrumbs are golden and crisp. Once you've turned the chicken over to fry the other side, heat another small frying pan over a medium-high heat and add another splash of oil. Fry the remaining egg.

5. Set the cooked chicken aside on a warm plate lined with kitchen paper to soak up any excess oil. Serve the chicken schnitzel with the egg and the anchovies on top and the capers sprinkled over.

STORECUPBOARD

2 teaspoons Dijon mustard

freshly ground sea salt and black pepper

2 tablespoons plain flour

light oil

2 anchovy fillets in olive oil

1 tablespoon nonpareille capers

FRESH

2 large eggs

3 tablespoons breadcrumbs

1 large chicken breast

QUICK LATE-NIGHT MISO SOUP

MAKES: 1 portion | **PREP TIME:** 5 minutes | **COOKING TIME:** 5 minutes

Sometimes you're home so late that, while you need something to eat, you don't have the time or the inclination to make a proper meal. This miso soup base can be finished with whatever fresh Asian ingredients and aromatics you may happen to have in the fridge. I've just included some of my favourites below by way of a guide. If you've got a bit more time on your hands, adding cooked noodles to the soup is always a good idea.

Keep a jar of brown rice miso in the fridge (which is also great mashed with butter and spread on corn on the cob), and you can have a warm and nourishing bowl of soup at any time, ready in minutes.

1. Put the kettle on to boil while you slice the mushrooms and chilli and trim and shred the spring onion. In the bottom of a mug or small soup bowl, mix together the miso and the soy sauce to create a paste. Fill the mug or bowl with boiling water, and stir until the miso has dissolved. Add the mushrooms, chilli, spring onion and coriander and enjoy instantly.

STORECUPBOARD

1 tablespoon dark soy sauce

FRESH

a small handful of shiitake mushrooms

1 small red chilli, sliced

1 large spring onion

2 teaspoons brown rice miso paste

a small handful of fresh coriander leaves

PEA, PRAWN & MUSHROOM EGG-FRIED RICE

MAKES: 1 portion | **PREP TIME:** 5 minutes | **COOKING TIME:** 10 minutes

Egg-fried rice makes a fantastic, satisfying, last-minute supper, especially if served with a couple of ice-cold beers. This is also one of those great-for-leftovers dishes; make it with leftover cooked rice (which shouldn't be kept for more than a day or two) and whatever prawns are still in the freezer, leftover pieces of roast chicken and any Asian vegetables you have to hand.

1. Heat 1 teaspoon of the oil in a wok or very large frying pan over a very high heat. Beat the egg, add to the pan and quickly scramble. Remove the egg from the pan, and set aside.

2. Heat the remaining teaspoon of oil and cook the mushrooms for a few minutes until they are slightly soft. Add the frozen peas, prawns and the sliced spring onions to the pan and cook until the prawns have defrosted. Add the rice and fry until everything is combined and the rice is thoroughly heated. Return the egg to the pan along with the soy sauce and sesame oil. Toss until all of the rice is well coated.

STORECUPBOARD

2 teaspoons light oil

1 tablespoon light soy sauce

FRESH

1 large egg

8 shiitake or chestnut mushrooms, sliced

a small handful of frozen peas or petits pois

a small handful of frozen cooked prawns

2 spring onions, trimmed and sliced

60g cooked and cold leftover rice

1 teaspoon toasted sesame oil

PAD THAI

MAKES: 1 portion | **PREP TIME**: 5 minutes | **COOKING TIME**: 15 minutes

Pad Thai was the first Thai dish I ever cooked and it is full of the flavours I crave if I'm after a big bowl of aromatic noodles. This recipe is the closest I've managed to get at home to the street Pad Thai they cook to order at the Brick Lane weekend indoor food market.

You can also make this with cooked pieces of chicken, and you can sub out the tamarind with fresh lime juice if you don't have any. I don't eat peanuts, but it is traditional to toast and chop a few to sprinkle over the finished dish.

1. Cook the rice noodles in a saucepan full of boiling water over a high heat until they are tender. I know the packet says to just leave them to soak in boiling water, but ignore this. I've never successfully managed to cook them in this way!

2. Meanwhile, make the rest of the stir-fry. Beat together the egg and spring onion and set a wok or the largest frying pan you have over a very high heat. Heat 1½ teaspoons of the oil until it is smoking and scramble the egg mixture. Remove from the pan, and return the pan to the heat.

3. Heat the rest of the oil (another 1½ teaspoons) and fry the beansprouts until they start to soften. Combine the fish sauce, tamarind paste, sugar and soy sauce, then add to the pan.

4. At this point the noodles should be cooked; drain them and run them under the cold tap for a couple of seconds to rinse off any excess starch. Add the noodles to the pan, along with the prawns. Once the prawns have heated through, transfer the pad Thai to a heated bowl. Sprinkle with fresh coriander, and serve with fresh lime wedges.

STORECUPBOARD

3 teaspoons light oil

½ teaspoon golden caster sugar

1 teaspoon dark soy sauce

FRESH

50g rice noodles

1 large egg

2 spring onions, trimmed and shredded

a large handful of beansprouts

2 tablespoons fish sauce

1 teaspoon tamarind paste

a large handful of frozen cooked prawns

fresh coriander, roughly chopped

lime wedges, to serve

CHICKEN NOODLE & OYSTER SAUCE STIR-FRY

MAKES: 1 portion | **PREP TIME:** 10 minutes | **COOKING TIME:** 15 minutes

During my year abroad, one of the things I treated myself to the first week in my new apartment was a wok so that I could whip up a last-minute stir-fry or two (I also used my wok to make the filling for Chicken Fajitas, page 126).

I know this is the only recipe in the book that uses oyster sauce, but I promise you that you'll keep using it. It really brings together any quick stir-fry of vegetables, protein and noodles, with no need for a recipe.

1. Combine the garlic with the oyster sauce, soy sauce, cornflour and sesame oil. Add the chicken and leave to marinate while you cook the noodles in a pan full of boiling water, set over a high heat, as per the packet instructions.

2. Heat the light oil in a wok or the largest frying pan you have over a very high heat. Add the chicken and cook for a minute or two until it is cooked through. Add the beansprouts and the sugar snaps to the pan, and stir fry until the sugar snaps are tender. Drain the noodles and add them to the wok, along with the spring onion. Stir until the noodles are well coated and serve straight away in a warm bowl.

STORECUPBOARD

1 large garlic clove, finely chopped

1 tablespoon dark soy sauce

1 nest of egg noodles

½ tablespoon light oil

FRESH

2 tablespoons oyster sauce

1 teaspoon cornflour

½ teaspoon toasted sesame oil

1 small chicken breast, chopped

2 handfuls of beansprouts

2 handfuls of sugar snap peas

1 large spring onion, trimmed and shredded

FOOD FOR FRIENDS

DINNER FOR TWO 116

FEASTS 126

SHARING STEAK WITH THYME-ROASTED CHERRY TOMATOES

SERVES: 2 | **PREP TIME:** 10 minutes | **COOKING TIME:** 25 minutes

Steak can be a bit pricey, but if you buy a cut like rump or sirloin without the bone, you can cut it into very thin slices to feed two of you for a date-night dinner with these easy thyme-roasted cherry tomatoes spooned over the top. Buy whatever you can afford, and look out for special offers. I like to keep a few steaks in the freezer as they defrost relatively quickly.

Serve with red wine, some sort of salad and fresh, rustic-style bread to mop up the juices.

1. Preheat the oven to 170°C/325°F/Gas mark 3.

2. Spread the tomatoes out, cut side up, in a baking tray. Drizzle them with the balsamic vinegar and extra virgin olive oil. Sprinkle with fresh thyme and season with freshly ground sea salt and black pepper. Roast in the oven for 25 minutes.

3. While the tomatoes are roasting, remove the steak from the fridge to bring it up to room temperature. Rub it with a little light oil, and season on both sides with salt and pepper.

4. Ten minutes before the tomatoes come out of the oven, heat a medium frying pan over a very high heat until the pan is smoking slightly. Fry the steak for a few minutes on each side until it is completely browned on the outside, but if you press the middle with your knuckles, it still feels squishy. This is the easiest way to tell that the steak is rare to medium rare.

5. Remove the steak from the pan to rest on a chopping board. Pour over any excess juices from the pan, and cover with a piece of tin foil to keep the heat in. Just before you're ready to serve, using the sharpest knife you have, cut the steak into very thin slices, slightly on the diagonal to create wider pieces. Divide these between two plates, pour over any resting juices from the chopping board, and spoon over the roasted cherry tomatoes.

STORECUPBOARD

1 teaspoon balsamic vinegar

1 teaspoon extra virgin olive oil

freshly ground sea salt and black pepper

light oil

FRESH

2 large handfuls of cherry tomatoes, halved

a small handful of fresh thyme leaves

1 steak

ROASTED RED PEPPERS WITH TOMATOES & ANCHOVIES

SERVES: 2 | **PREP TIME:** 10 minutes | **COOKING TIME:** 1 hour 20 minutes

STORECUPBOARD

4 large garlic cloves, thinly sliced

freshly ground sea salt and black pepper

8 anchovy fillets in olive oil

extra virgin olive oil

FRESH

2 large red peppers

3–4 large handfuls of cherry tomatoes, halved

I've got my mother to thank for helping me fall in love with this Italian classic; it is one of her go-to summer dishes. Use the ripest, reddest tomatoes you can find, and serve with generous amounts of fresh crusty bread and ice-cold rosé.

1. Preheat the oven to 180°C/350°F/Gas mark 4.

2. Cut the peppers in half and remove the seeds, keeping the stalks intact. Lay them, cut side up, in a shallow baking dish.

3. Fill the pepper cavities with the cherry tomatoes. Sprinkle the slices of garlic over the tomato-filled peppers. Lay two anchovy fillets on top of each pepper half and season with salt and black pepper.

4. Drizzle the peppers generously with extra virgin olive oil, and roast in the oven for 1 hour 20 minutes, or until the peppers are tender.

CLASSIC MOULES MARINIÈRES

SERVES: 2 | **PREP TIME**: 25 minutes | **COOKING TIME**: 10 minutes

Moules marinières is, hands down, one of my favourite dishes, and is super-easy to make. It is the perfect dinner for two if you're looking to impress, served with some nice white wine and fresh crusty bread to mop up the juices.

Don't let the amount of preparation time put you off – 25 minutes is the longest you'll spend scrubbing and de-bearding the mussels if you've purchased a particularly gnarly (but still delicious) bag of them. Usually they only take me about 10 to 15 minutes to do.

1. To prepare the mussels, clear the kitchen sink, put in the plug and fill it with cold water. Fill a large bowl with cold water too. Tip the mussels into the sink and, using a clean sponge, scrub off any excess barnacles and try to tear off as many of the scraggly 'beards' that may be attached to the mussels. If any shells are cracked, throw the mussels away. Also, if any mussels are open, hold them closed for about 30 seconds. If the mussels stay closed, they're fine to eat. If they don't, throw them away. As you clean the mussels, transfer them to the bowl of cold water while you work on the rest.

2. Heat the butter in the largest, lidded saucepan you have over a medium heat until it is frothy. Cook the shallots for a few minutes until they are tender, and add the wine, a small glass of water and a generous seasoning of salt and pepper.

3. Drain the mussels and add them to the pan. Add the lid and steam the mussels for 5 minutes, shaking the pan occasionally. The mussels should steam open.

4. Add the chopped parsley, and shake the pan again with the lid on. Divide the mussels between two bowls, throwing away any shells that have not opened. Serve straight away with another bowl for the discarded shells.

STORECUPBOARD

freshly ground sea salt and black pepper

FRESH

500g mussels

a very large knob of butter

2 banana shallots, finely chopped

1 small glass white wine

a small handful of fresh flat-leaf parsley, chopped

SAUSAGES WITH MUSTARD MASH & ONION GRAVY

SERVES: 2 | **PREP TIME:** 10 minutes | **COOKING TIME:** 25–30 minutes

It only takes half an hour to make two platefuls of piping hot, juicy sausages nestled on a bed of mustard-mashed potatoes and finished off with a generous amount of homemade onion gravy. So obviously this is what you'll want to make for dinner after class when you've had to walk home in the rain.

1. Preheat the oven to 200°C/400°F/Gas mark 6.

2. Put the potatoes in a medium saucepan with a generous amount of salt and enough cold water to cover the potatoes. Set them to boil over a high heat for 20 to 25 minutes until tender.

3. Meanwhile, pierce the sausages in a couple of places with a sharp knife and cook them in the oven for 15 to 20 minutes in an ovenproof dish.

4. To make the onion gravy, heat the oil and a large knob of the butter in a medium frying pan until frothy. Add the onion and cook, stirring occasionally, for 15 minutes until the onion has softened and is starting to go golden. Add the sugar and cook for another 5 minutes. Stir in the flour, stock, Dijon mustard, a good splash of Worcestershire sauce and some salt and pepper. Allow to bubble away for another 5 to 10 minutes until you're ready to eat.

5. When the potatoes are cooked, drain away the water and mash with the wholegrain mustard, milk and another very large knob of butter. Season to taste with salt and pepper. Pile everything onto a warm plate, and enjoy.

STORECUPBOARD

a splash of light oil

2 onions, thinly sliced

a large pinch of golden caster sugar

½ teaspoon plain flour

200ml vegetable stock (made with ½ stock cube)

½ teaspoon Dijon mustard

Worcestershire sauce

freshly ground sea salt and black pepper

2 teaspoons wholegrain mustard

FRESH

2 large potatoes, peeled and quartered

4 sausages

unsalted butter

2 tablespoons milk

SAUSAGE ROAST WITH MUSTARD SOURED CREAM

SERVES: 2 | PREP TIME: 10 minutes | COOKING TIME: 40 minutes

This is a great way to use up slightly soft apples and stale bread. It provides a comforting, filling supper for two on a blustery wet autumn evening. The mustard soured cream is optional, but highly recommended.

Any mildly flavoured cooking oil is fine here, but I prefer to use cold-pressed rapeseed oil as it adds an extra grassy flavour to the sweet roast leeks.

1. Preheat the oven to 180°C/350°F/Gas mark 4.

2. Toss the red onions, leeks and apples in the oil and a generous amount of salt and pepper. You can either do this in a large roasting dish or in a sealed plastic bag to make sure all of the pieces are super-coated in the seasoned oil. Cook in the roasting dish for 15 minutes.

3. Meanwhile, to make the mustard soured cream stir together the soured cream and wholegrain and Dijon mustards. Add a little bit of sea salt to taste.

4. Toss the vegetables and apples around in the roasting dish and then add the sausages. With the tip of a sharp knife pierce each sausage in a couple of places, and return to the oven to cook for a further 15 minutes.

5. Tear or cut up some leftover bread to create a couple of handfuls of rough croutons. Nestle these around the vegetables, apples and sausages and roast for a final 10 minutes until the bread has started to toast. Serve with the mustard soured cream.

STORECUPBOARD

2 red onions, cut into wedges

2 tablespoons light oil

freshly ground sea salt and black pepper

2 teaspoons wholegrain mustard

1 teaspoon Dijon mustard

FRESH

2 leeks, trimmed and cut into chunks

2 eating apples, cored and cut into wedges

4 tablespoons soured cream

4 sausages

leftover stale bread

ONE-PAN CHICKEN ROAST WITH AUTUMN VEGETABLES

SERVES: 2 | **PREP TIME:** 15 minutes | **COOKING TIME:** 45 minutes

While everyone loves a good roast dinner, wouldn't it be great if you could cook an entire roast in one pan, in one hour, from prep to table? I promise you that this recipe will change your roasting game forever.

This is easily doubled up to serve more people – you'll just need as big a roasting tray as you can fit in the oven as otherwise you'll end up with the vegetables steaming rather than roasting if you overcrowd the pan. Also, while I've made this recipe with many different vegetables, you can just mix and match depending on what you have in the fridge, making sure you cut everything to about the same size.

1. Preheat the oven to 200°C/400°F/Gas mark 6.

2. Peel the butternut squash, scrape the seeds out with a spoon and cut into equal-sized chunks. You don't need to peel the sweet potato, parsnips or carrots before chopping them. Cut the sweet potato and the parsnips into chunks like the squash, but you'll need to slice the carrots on the diagonal to create more surface area as they take a little longer to cook.

3. Either in a sealed plastic bag or in the roasting tray you're going to roast your vegetables in, toss the vegetables, along with the onions and garlic, in 1 tablespoon of oil and a generous amount of salt and pepper. If you're using the bag method, transfer the vegetables to the roasting tray.

4. Nestle the chicken thighs, skin side up, among the vegetables. Rub the skins with a little more oil and season with a bit more salt and pepper. Roast in the oven for 45 minutes.

STORECUPBOARD	FRESH
2 red onions, cut into wedges	½ butternut squash
4 garlic cloves, halved	1 small sweet potato
light oil	2 parsnips
freshly ground sea salt and black pepper	2 carrots
	4 skin-on, bone-in chicken thighs

ONE-PAN CHICKEN ROAST WITH SUMMER VEGETABLES

SERVES: 2 | PREP TIME: 10 minutes | COOKING TIME: 45 minutes

This is the summer version of my One-Pan Chicken Roast with Root Vegetables (opposite). It is lighter and brighter for the summer months, and is best served with a cold glass of wine and lots of fresh, crusty bread to mop up the juices from the plate.

Again, you can mix and match the vegetables. Some people like it when I throw a few black olives in the pan, and even pieces of fresh lemon, skin still intact, roast up beautifully here if you have any that need using up.

1. Preheat the oven to 200°C/400°F/Gas mark 6.

2. Cut the peppers and courgettes into even chunks. Toss everything apart from the chicken in 1 tablespoon of oil, either in a plastic bag or in the roasting tray you'll be using, and season well with salt and pepper. If you're using the bag method, tip the vegetables into the roasting tray.

3. Nestle the chicken thighs, skin side up, among the vegetables. Rub the skins with a little more oil, and season with a bit more salt and pepper. Roast in the oven for 45 minutes.

STORECUPBOARD	FRESH
2 red onions, cut into wedges	1 yellow pepper, deseeded
4 garlic cloves, halved	1 red pepper, deseeded
light oil	2 courgettes
freshly ground sea salt and black pepper	4 skin-on, bone-in chicken thighs

CHICKEN FAJITAS WITH SALSA & BOOZY GUACAMOLE

SERVES: 4 | **PREP TIME**: 15 minutes, plus 30 minutes chilling | **COOKING TIME**: 15 minutes

Fajitas are my favourite thing to serve up on a Saturday night for friends with a few beer margaritas (page 174). I love that everyone can build their own wraps from a selection of whatever you've provided. I like to serve up a selection of homemade Pico de Gallo Salsa, Boozy Guacamole, soured cream, grated cheese and black beans.

This recipe also works brilliantly with strips of steak (one steak between two people) and raw king prawns (a large handful per person). Just adjust the cooking time so that the meat or prawns are just cooked through. You can also make a veggie version by doubling up the vegetables and adding the marinade to the pan halfway through cooking.

If you can't find jalapeños for the salsa, you'll still have a delicious bowlful if you leave it out.

1. Combine the juice of the lime with the chilli powder, cumin, paprika, cayenne pepper, oregano and 1 teaspoon of the oil in a small bowl. Add the chicken breasts to the marinade, mixing everything until the chicken is completely coated. Leave to marinate in the fridge for at least half an hour.

2. To make the salsa, combine the onion and tomatoes in a small bowl, along with a generous pinch of sea salt. Add the jalapeño and coriander to the salsa and chill until needed.

3. When you're ready to cook, take the chicken out of the fridge to come up to room temperature. Do the same with the salsa.

4. At this stage, you'll be able to make the guacamole without having to worry about it going brown before you eat. Peel and mash the avocados and mix in the soured cream. Add the red onion and stir it in, along with a splash of tequila. Season to taste with fresh lime juice and sea salt.

5. Heat a wok or the largest frying pan you have over a very high heat. Heat the remaining teaspoon of oil and add the peppers and onions. Stir-fry for 6 to 8 minutes until the peppers and onions have started to soften and they are charring around the edges.

6. Add the chicken and all of the marinade juices to the pan and carry on stir-frying for 7 to 8 minutes until the chicken is cooked through. Bring to the table in a heated bowl with the tortilla wraps, guacamole, salsa and any other fillings.

FOR THE FAJITAS:

STORECUPBOARD

2 teaspoons chilli powder

½ teaspoon ground cumin

½ teaspoon dried oregano

2 teaspoons light oil

2 white onions, cut into chunks

FRESH

juice of 1 lime

½ teaspoon sweet smoked paprika

¼ teaspoon cayenne pepper

2 large chicken breasts, sliced into thin strips

1 red pepper, deseeded and sliced

1 yellow pepper, deseeded and sliced

8 tortilla wraps

FOR THE PICO DE GALLO SALSA:

STORECUPBOARD

½ white onion, finely chopped

sea salt

FRESH

2 large tomatoes, finely chopped

1 jalapeño pepper, deseeded and finely chopped

a small handful of fresh coriander, roughly chopped

FOR THE BOOZY GUACAMOLE:

STORECUPBOARD

½ red onion, finely chopped

sea salt

FRESH

2 large ripe avocados

2 tablespoons soured cream

a splash of tequila

lime juice

EASY ROOT VEGETABLE CURRY

SERVES: 4 | **PREP TIME**: 15 minutes | **COOKING TIME**: 1 hour 5 minutes

I got in on cooking Indian food for myself pretty late in the game. When my friend Amy found out about my newfound love, she sent me an email containing what she called 'the only curry recipe you'll ever need'. I've changed Amy's version up a bit to suit my personal tastes and the types of ingredients I usually have hanging around, but I absolutely agree that once you've got this curry in your repertoire, you're set.

If I don't use a whole tin of coconut milk in one recipe, I like to keep it in a clean, empty screw-top bottle in the fridge to add a little creaminess to soups or to make Coconut Hot Chocolate (page 170).

This curry is delicious served with rice or naan or both. Finish each bowl with a sprinkling of chopped fresh coriander. Also, I like to add a star anise and a splash more coconut milk in with the rice as it cooks for a little bit of extra flavour.

1. Preheat the oven to 200°C/400°F/Gas mark 6.

2. Cut whatever vegetables and potatoes you're using into roughly 2cm cubes. Spread the cubed vegetables and the garlic out in a baking tray and toss together with a light drizzle of oil and the cumin. Roast for about 20 minutes, until the vegetables that cook the fastest are just about tender. It does not matter if some of the vegetables, such as the potatoes, are still a bit firm; they'll keep on cooking in the sauce.

3. Meanwhile, heat another splash of oil in the bottom of a large saucepan over a medium heat. Fry the onion with the turmeric, coriander and a good pinch of chilli flakes until the onion is soft and you can smell the spices wafting out of the pan. Stir in the tomato purée, followed by the coconut milk.

4. Bring to the boil, then reduce the heat and allow the sauce to bubble away for a couple of minutes. Add the stock and stir, making sure to scrape off any burnt-on bits at the bottom of the pan. Add the ginger and roasted vegetables. Turn up the heat to high, and let the curry bubble away for about 5 minutes, uncovered.

5. Season with a good pinch of salt and turn the heat down to low, covering with a lid. Leave to simmer for 40 minutes. Stir occasionally to check it is not thickening too much and it is not drying out (it will depend on what vegetables you use; you can add a little bit more water if necessary).

6. Before serving, check you are happy with the flavours. You can add a bit more salt if you think it needs it, or tomato purée for a touch of acidity.

STORECUPBOARD

2 large garlic cloves, thickly sliced

light oil

2½ tablespoons ground cumin

2 onions, chopped

a pinch of dried chilli flakes

400ml vegetable stock (made with 1 stock cube)

sea salt

FRESH

400g mixed root vegetables (potatoes, sweet potatoes, butternut squash)

1 tablespoon ground turmeric

2 teaspoons ground coriander

5 tablespoons tomato purée

100ml coconut milk

½ tablespoon chopped fresh ginger

PORK SOUVLAKI WITH LIGHT TZATZIKI & PITTA BREAD

SERVES: 4–6 | **PREP TIME**: 15 minutes, plus 2 hours marinating | **COOKING TIME**: 10 minutes

If you've eaten souvlaki recently, you might think it unusual that I'm using pork belly here. I've found that pieces of cubed pork shoulder dry out too quickly if you're cooking under the grill rather than on a barbecue, so be warned if you're tempted to substitute. Be sure to trim any bits of pork fat that are more than 5mm wide before cubing the belly slices so that your souvlaki are not too fatty.

Finally, shall I tell you what is the best thing about this recipe? You can freeze this in its marinade.

1. Grind a little bit of salt on top of the garlic pieces and run the flat edge of a large knife over them to crush to a paste. Combine the crushed garlic, oregano, lemon juice, olive oil, vinegar and a generous seasoning of sea salt and black pepper in a small bowl, and transfer the marinade to a large plastic bag.

2. Trim the pork belly slices and cut into manageable chunks. Add to the marinade and tie a knot in the top of the plastic bag, pushing out as much air as possible. Once the bag is sealed, massage the pork belly until it is well coated in the marinade and leave in the fridge for at least 2 hours, but preferably overnight.

3. Preheat the grill to 250°C/485°F or as hot as it will go. Divide the pork belly pieces between eight wooden skewers and grill for 5 minutes on each side. If you're a washing-up dodger like me, line the bottom of the grill pan with foil first.

4. Serve straight away with warmed pittas, some salad leaves and tzatziki.

STORECUPBOARD

2 garlic cloves, chopped

freshly ground sea salt and black pepper

2 tablespoons dried oregano

8 tablespoons extra virgin olive oil

2 teaspoons red wine vinegar

FRESH

juice of 2 lemons

10 pork belly slices

pittas, to serve

salad leaves, to serve

1 portion of Light Tzatziki (page 78), to serve

SPICED LAMB PATTIES WITH LIGHT TZATZIKI & PITTA BREAD

SERVES: 4 | **PREP TIME:** 15 minutes | **COOKING TIME:** 20 minutes

A Greek supper of flavoured meat, tzatziki and salad stuffed into warm pitta is a fantastic thing to serve up for friends. However, not everyone eats pork, which means my Pork Souvlaki (opposite) won't always be a suitable option. This is where these wonderful spiced lamb patties come in. I find them slightly addictive, and this coming from someone who ordinarily does not even like lamb.

On the subject of substitutions, you can always serve up skewers of grilled vegetables (red onion, red and yellow peppers, courgette, aubergine chunks, etc.), brushed with olive oil, seasoned with salt and pepper and sprinkled with dried oregano as a veggie option.

1. Preheat the oven to 200°C/400°F/Gas mark 6.

2. Combine the lamb, red onion, mint, cumin, lemon zest and a generous amount of freshly ground sea salt and black pepper until all of the herbs, onion and spices are evenly distributed throughout the mince.

3. Shape the mixture into roughly 10 to 12 patties and bake on a foil-lined baking tray for 20 minutes.

4. Serve straight away with warmed pittas, some salad leaves and tzatziki.

STORECUPBOARD	FRESH
1 small red onion, finely chopped	1 x 500g pack lamb mince
3 teaspoons ground cumin	a large handful of fresh mint, chopped
freshly ground sea salt and black pepper	zest of ½ lemon
	pittas, to serve
	salad leaves, to serve
	1 portion of Light Tzatziki (page 78), to serve

SUPER-EASY MEAT-FREE MIXED BEAN CHILLI

SERVES: 3–4 | **PREP TIME:** 5 minutes | **COOKING TIME:** 55 minutes

Chilli recipes are very personal. I know everyone has their own secret method and ingredients, so all I can do here is share how I make mine. While the combination of spices and beans you choose is important, for me a bowl of chilli is not a bowl of chilli if I have not loaded it up with avocado, soured cream, fresh coriander and a good spritz of fresh lime juice. It is a great way to use up whatever you have left in the bottom of your fridge. Grated cheese, chopped red onion, fresh salsa and cold shredded chicken are also perfect here to add a bit more flavour and texture.

1. Heat a good splash of oil over a medium-high heat in a large saucepan, and fry the onion and the pepper pieces for 7 to 8 minutes until they are soft and just starting to brown.

2. Empty the red kidney beans and the black beans into a sieve and rinse under cold water. Add them to the pan, along with the tomatoes, spice mix, cumin and cocoa powder. Use a little water to rinse out the tomato tin so you don't leave any of the tomato goodness behind, and add about 200ml water in total to the pan.

3. Stir well and turn up the heat until the chilli is bubbling. Reduce the heat to low and allow to simmer, without a lid and stirring occasionally, for 20 minutes.

4. Rinse the lentils in a sieve under cold water until the water runs clear, and stir them into the chilli. Allow to simmer for another 25 minutes, still stirring occasionally, until the lentils are plump and tender and the chilli has thickened.

STORECUPBOARD

light oil

2 white onions, cut into small chunks

1 x 400g tin chopped tomatoes

½ teaspoon ground cumin

1 teaspoon cocoa powder

FRESH

1 yellow pepper, deseeded and cut into small chunks

1 x 400g tin red kidney beans

1 x 400g tin black beans

1½ tablespoons Cajun spice mix

5 heaped tablespoons red split lentils

BACON & BEAN HOT POT

SERVES: 3–4 | **PREP TIME:** 10 minutes | **COOKING TIME:** 45 minutes

This is perfect as a filling spring supper with a green salad on the side for those days that are sunny but still a bit crisp and cold. While I love the rich, smoky flavour the lardons add to the beans, you've also got a pretty decent veggie answer to this English classic here if you leave them out all together.

1. Heat a splash of oil in a large saucepan over a medium heat.

2. Once the oil is shimmering, fry the carrot and the onion until they are softened, but not golden. Add the garlic, and cook for another few minutes until the garlic has softened. Add the bacon lardons and fry until they are cooked through.

3. Add the beans, chopped tomatoes and the ½ stock cube made up in the empty tomato tin with half a tin's worth of boiling water. Season well with salt and pepper and a large pinch of sugar. Bring to the boil, then reduce the heat to medium-low and allow to simmer, stirring occasionally, for 20 minutes.

4. Meanwhile, preheat the grill to 220°C/425°F. Thinly slice the potato and cook in a saucepan of salted boiling water for 5 minutes until the potato slices are tender, but still hold their shape.

5. Transfer the bean mixture to an ovenproof baking dish, and spread the potato slices over the top. Season with a few grinds of salt and pepper, and drizzle with a little oil. Grill for 15 minutes, until the potatoes are golden and slightly crispy.

STORECUPBOARD

light oil

1 white onion, chopped

2 garlic cloves, chopped

1 x 400g tin chopped tomatoes

½ vegetable stock cube

freshly ground sea salt and black pepper

a pinch of golden caster sugar

FRESH

2 carrots, peeled and chopped

1 x 90g pack smoked bacon lardons

2 x 400g tins mixed beans, drained

1 very large baking potato

SAUSAGE BOLOGNESE

SERVES: 4 | **PREP TIME:** 20 minutes | **COOKING TIME:** 1 hour 10 minutes

I love a good bolognese sauce. Yes, you can eat it with pasta, sprinkled with fresh basil, and stash any leftovers in the freezer for days when you don't fancy cooking, but it also creates a great base for so many other comforting dishes. Make this on a Sunday evening just for yourself, and you'll then have enough bolognese left to make a Frying-Pan Lasagne (page 95) or to fill a couple of baked potatoes (page 105) midweek.

I use sausage meat here because not only is it cheaper than beef or lamb mince, but it adds enough of that pork flavour so that you don't have to fork out for bacon to add to your bolognese, too.

1. Heat a generous splash of light oil in the bottom of a large saucepan over a medium heat. When the oil is shimmering, add the onion, carrot and celery. Cook for about 5 minutes until the pieces have started to soften, but they have not yet started to brown.

2. Add the garlic and cook for another 2 minutes until the garlic is soft, but again, don't let it start to brown (brown garlic is burnt garlic).

3. Add the sausage meat, breaking it into pieces with the back of your mixing spoon, stirring every few minutes. The sausage meat should start to break up like minced meat as it cooks.

4. Once the sausage meat is cooked through, add the stock, wine, tinned tomatoes, tomato purée, oregano, a good pinch of sugar and a generous seasoning of salt and black pepper. To get the last of the goodness out of the tomato tin, pour a little of the wine or stock into the tin and swill it around before adding it to the saucepan.

5. Bring to the boil, then reduce the heat to low, and allow the sauce to simmer, without a lid, for 55 minutes. In the last 10 minutes of cooking, taste a little of the sauce to check the seasoning. Add more pepper if you think it needs a bit more flavour. More salt will help if you think the sauce tastes a little bland, and a bit more sugar will round out the sauce if it tastes too acidic.

STORECUPBOARD

light oil

1 small white onion, finely chopped

2 large garlic cloves, finely chopped

100ml chicken or beef stock (made with ½ stock cube)

1 x 400g tin chopped tomatoes

2 teaspoons dried oregano

a large pinch of golden caster sugar

freshly ground sea salt and black pepper

FRESH

1 large carrot, peeled and finely chopped

1 celery stick, finely chopped

450g sausage meat

230ml red wine

1 tablespoon tomato purée

TOAD IN THE HOLE WITH ONION GRAVY

MAKES: 6 | **PREP TIME**: 5 minutes | **COOKING TIME**: 25 minutes

You can always take these ingredients and cook them in one roasting tin to make a traditional toad in the hole. However, I think these dinky little single-serve portions are so much better, especially if you're cooking for friends and you want dinner to look far more impressive than it actually is. Serve with Onion Gravy and Mustard Mash (page 120).

1. Preheat the oven as high as it will go, about 240°C/475°F/Gas mark 9.

2. Pour ½ tablespoon of oil into each hole of a large muffin tin and put it in the oven so the oil can heat up.

3. Heat a splash of oil in a large frying pan. Fry the chipolatas for a few minutes until they are golden brown, but not cooked in the middle.

4. In a jug or bowl, whisk together the eggs and the milk until combined. Gradually whisk in the flour until smooth and then season with salt and black pepper.

5. Carefully remove the muffin tin from the oven and divide the batter between each oil-filled hole. Place a chipolata in each and return to the oven for 15 to 20 minutes, until the mini toad in the holes are puffy and golden.

STORECUPBOARD	FRESH
light oil	6 chipolata sausages
125g plain flour	2 large eggs
freshly ground sea salt and black pepper	150ml milk
	Mustard Mash and Onion Gravy (page 120), to serve

SWEET POTATO & SAUSAGE SHEPHERD'S PIE

SERVES: 6 | **PREP TIME:** 10 minutes | **COOKING TIME:** 35–45 minutes

Shepherd's pie is one of those things that will always be better homemade. I like the sweet potato topping for something a little different, but if you want to go for a more classic flavour, use regular potatoes instead.

If you'd like to make this with leftover bolognese, simply decrease the quantities for the mashed sweet potato and bake in a smaller dish.

1. Preheat the oven to 200°C/400°F/Gas mark 6.

2. Boil the sweet potato slices in salted boiling water for 15 to 20 minutes until tender. Drain, then mash with a potato masher until smooth, adding the milk and the butter as you go. Season generously with salt and pepper.

3. Spread the bolognese sauce (it does not matter if it is hot from the pan or cold from the fridge) over the bottom of an ovenproof dish and spoon the mashed sweet potato evenly over the top. Spread out with a knife until all of the sauce is covered, and season the top with a little more salt and pepper.

4. Bake in the oven for 20 to 25 minutes, until the sweet potato top has started to go crispy and slightly brown, and the bolognese sauce has started to bubble up around the edges.

STORECUPBOARD

freshly ground sea salt and black pepper

FRESH

3 (roughly 850g) sweet potatoes, peeled and sliced into 1cm discs

6 tablespoons milk

30g unsalted butter

4 portions of Sausage Bolognese (page 134)

EASY LEMON & THYME ROAST CHICKEN WITH ZA'ATAR POTATOES

SERVES: 4–5 | **PREP TIME:** 10 minutes, plus 10 minutes resting | **COOKING TIME:** as per the packet instructions (approximately 1 hour 45 minutes)

Everyone needs a good, basic roast chicken recipe in their back pocket. On Sunday nights there is nothing better than a glorious, golden bird being carried from the oven to the table to share, with the added bonus of cold leftover chicken to devour in sandwiches or a pie (page 140) during the week. Buy a large chicken if you want extra leftovers!

While my family go down the traditional roast potato and steamed vegetable route, I like to serve my chicken with za'atar potatoes or potato wedges, mayonnaise (rather than making gravy) and a simple green salad.

1. Take the chicken out of the fridge at least half an hour before you want to cook it to bring it up to room temperature. Meanwhile, preheat the oven to 200°C/400°F/Gas mark 6.

2. Remove the chicken from all of its packaging, and remove any string trussing it together. Place the chicken on a wire rack set inside a deep roasting tray. If you don't have anything suitable, you can keep the chicken off the base of the tin by thickly slicing a couple of onions to create a trivet to rest the chicken on. This will also help you make an awesome gravy (see opposite).

3. Pat dry the skin of the chicken with kitchen paper. Using a sharp knife, pierce the lemon all over and halve it. Stuff the lemon halves, along with the thyme sprigs, into the chicken cavity. If possible, fold over any excess skin at the neck to shut the lemon and herbs in.

4. Rub the skin of the chicken with butter, and season generously with salt and pepper.

5. Roast the chicken as per the packet instructions. No two chickens weigh the same, so they'll usually have a cooking time printed on the packaging.

6. Boil the potatoes in salted boiling water for 15 to 20 minutes until they're tender. Once the potatoes are cool enough to touch, halve them and toss them in a plastic bag with the oil, za'atar and a generous amount of salt and pepper. Tip them into a roasting tray and put them in the oven to roast with the chicken for the last 30 minutes of cooking.

7. When the chicken is cooked, the skin should be golden and crispy, and if you poke a sharp knife into a thick bit of the chicken (not the breast) the juices that run out should be completely clear.

8. Leave the chicken to rest on a chopping or carving board for 10 minutes before carving.

STORECUPBOARD

freshly ground sea salt and black pepper

1 tablespoon light oil

FRESH

1 large whole chicken (approximately 1.2 kg)

1 large lemon

a large handful of fresh thyme sprigs

a large knob of butter, at room temperature

1 x 500g pack new potatoes

1 tablespoon za'atar

How to make pan gravy: While the chicken is resting is a great opportunity to make gravy. Before you lift the chicken out of the roasting tray, turn it on its end so that any cooking juices from inside the chicken, infused with lemon and thyme, can run out into the tin.

Spoon out as much fat floating on top of the liquid still in the roasting tray as you can, and set the tin over a medium heat. If you've made an onion trivet to rest your chicken on, mash this down to a purée with a fork and remove the skins from the pan.

Using a fork or a metal whisk, while the juices warm up, scrape off as much of the burnt-on bits from the bottom of the tin. This is where most of the flavour is hiding! Add splashes of water (my Dad likes to use any water he's cooking vegetables in), wine or a mixture of both to the tin to create more liquid as it evaporates.

To thicken the gravy, mix a little cornflour into some water, and then gradually whisk this into the gravy pan until you've reached the desired consistency. Season to taste with salt and pepper.

LEFTOVER ROAST CHICKEN PIE

SERVES: 6 | **PREP TIME:** 25 minutes | **COOKING TIME:** 45 minutes

Use whatever chicken you have left over from your Sunday bird. You need about three large handfuls, but a bit more will just make a meatier pie (or you could keep some back to make sandwiches), and if you don't quite have enough, just use a few more mushrooms to pad the pie out.

This is a great dish either to serve up with some potato wedges and a salad if you've got friends coming over for a midweek supper, or to make for just one or two of you. The only thing I like more than this freshly made roast chicken pie is this cold leftover roast chicken pie!

1. Heat the butter in a large frying pan over a medium high heat. Add the leek chunks and cook them until they start to soften and brown around the edges.

2. Add the mushrooms and bacon to the pan, and continue to cook until the bacon has cooked through and the mushrooms have softened and started to brown. While they are cooking, toss the chicken in the flour with a generous amount of salt and pepper.

3. Add the chicken and flour mixture to the pan, and stir in until the flour has formed a very thick paste. Depending on how much chicken you're using, the pan may be getting a bit full at this point, but don't worry! It won't affect the flavour and nothing will over- or undercook.

4. Stir in the stock, followed by the cream and white wine or water. Bring to the boil, then reduce the heat to low and allow the sauce to bubble away until it is a little thicker than a pie filling would usually be. From start to finish, the filling should take about 20 minutes to cook.

5. Remove the pan from the heat and leave the filling to cool a little. Preheat the oven to 200°C/400°F/Gas mark 6 and place a metal baking tray in the oven to heat up too. Baking the pie on a preheated metal tray will help you avoid a soggy bottom.

6. Halve the pastry block. Using a rolling pin or a bottle of wine, roll out one of the halves on a clean work surface (sprinkled with a little flour) until it is thick enough to line a 22cm pie dish, or any other ovenproof dish you could line and top with pastry, and big enough to hold the pie filling. Line the dish with the pastry. I've found the easiest way to do this is to slide your rolling pin or wine bottle under the pastry sheet to help you lift the pastry up so you can slide the pie dish underneath. Don't worry if you don't get it first time; it takes practice!

7. Roll out the other half of the pastry block so it is big enough to top the pie. Spoon the pie filling into the dish.

STORECUPBOARD

1 tablespoon plain flour, plus extra for dusting

freshly ground sea salt and black pepper

200ml chicken stock (made with ½ stock cube)

FRESH

a large knob of unsalted butter

2 leeks, trimmed and cut into 3cm chunks

8 mushrooms, sliced

4 rashers of bacon, cut into small pieces (I find this is easiest to do with scissors)

leftover roast chicken (page 138)

1 x 150ml pot single cream

a generous glug of white wine or water

1 x 375g block puff pastry

1 tablespoon milk

8. Brush the edges of the pastry with the milk, and lay the second pastry sheet on top. Lift the pie up in the air. This makes it easier to slice the excess pastry off from around the sides of the pie dish. Make a thumbprint pattern around the edge of the pie to seal the pastry. You can use any pastry scraps to decorate the top.

9. Brush the pie lid with milk, and bake it in the oven for 25 minutes until the pastry is golden. Leave the pie to stand for 10 minutes before serving.

SOME-THING SWEET

CAKES, COOKIES & SNACKS 144

PUDDINGS 154

HONEYCOMB CRUNCH REFRIGERATOR SQUARES

MAKES: 12 squares | **PREP TIME:** 5 minutes, plus 1 hour chilling | **COOKING TIME:** 5 minutes

Piled up on a plate in the fridge, these are super-addictive. I like to grab one if I'm after something sweet after a big meal, or for a mid-afternoon pick-me-up.

Feel free to chop and change the ingredients a little: the honey/butter/chocolate base is the starting point for a whole world of different possibilities. Add mini marshmallows, raisins and glacé cherries for an easy rocky road.

1. Measure the butter, honey and salt into a saucepan and set over a medium heat. Stir until the butter has completely melted and combined with the honey. Add the chocolate to the pan, and stir until it is all melted and the mixture is smooth.

2. Break up the biscuits and the honeycomb bars into chunks. Stir into the chocolate mixture until everything is coated.

3. Line the bottom of a loaf tin, baking tray or brownie tin with a double layer of cling film. If you're using one of the larger types of tin, you may want to double the amount here, or press the mix into only half the tin to avoid making super-thin and fragile bars. Press the mixture into the prepared tray, and chill in the fridge for at least an hour.

4. Once the mixture is solid, turn it out of the tin, remove the cling film and slice the slab into 12 small squares. Store in the fridge for up to a week, if they even last that long!

STORECUPBOARD

2 tablespoons runny honey

a pinch of salt

50g plain chocolate, chopped

FRESH

50g unsalted butter

7 digestive biscuits (approximately 100g)

3 chocolate-coated honeycomb bars (approximately 100g)

ORANGE CHOCOLATE CHIP COOKIES

MAKES: 10 cookies | **PREP TIME:** 15 minutes | **COOKING TIME:** 10–12 minutes

Everyone loves a good chocolate chip cookie. While I used to be all about the triple or quadruple chip cookie, stuffed with every type of chocolate and enriched with cocoa powder, these days I'm after something a bit more refined. A dusting of orange zest and a couple of handfuls of dark chocolate chips now make these my favourite cookie. Oh, and did I mention that they only take half an hour to make?

This is also a good base recipe for additions. I love to make bright and colourful M&M cookies by switching out the chocolate for M&M's, and the orange zest for ½ teaspoon vanilla extract.

1. Preheat the oven to 170°C/325°F/Gas mark 3 and line two baking trays with baking parchment. If you only have one tray, you can bake these cookies in two batches.

2. In a mixing bowl and using a mixing spoon, beat together the butter and sugar until the mixture is light and fluffy. Beat in the orange zest and the egg until the mixture is smooth.

3. Add the baking powder, salt and flour, and mix until everything is just combined – overmixing the dough will result in tough cookies. Fold in the chocolate chips.

4. Divide the mixture into 10 balls (they will flatten and spread during cooking) and arrange them on the baking trays. Bake in the oven for 10 to 12 minutes until the cookies are golden and, when pressed with a fingertip, they are still soft, but definitely cooked in the middle.

5. Leave the cookies on the baking tray for a couple of minutes to harden a little before sliding them off onto a wire rack to cool.

Getting the perfect cookies: There is a thin line between getting a nice, chewy cookie with a soft middle that hardens up as the cookie cools, and a doughy one that's still raw in the middle. It may sound hard, but I promise they'll come out perfect the second time if they don't the first! The temperature of your particular oven has a lot to do with it, and you'll get to know your oven over time.

STORECUPBOARD

½ teaspoon baking powder

a pinch of salt

200g plain flour

FRESH

150g unsalted butter, at room temperature

150g soft light brown sugar

zest of 1 orange

1 large egg

150g dark chocolate chips

BANANA & NUTELLA MUFFINS

MAKES: 6 muffins | **PREP TIME:** 15 minutes | **COOKING TIME:** 20 minutes

These muffins are great when freshly baked, so that the Nutella is still gooey. You can eat them at any time of day, but I do like them for an indulgent weekend breakfast as they only take 25 minutes to throw together. They're best the day you make them, but they freshen up well in the oven for a few minutes.

1. Preheat the oven to 180°C/350°F/Gas mark 4.

2. Combine the flour, baking powder, salt and sugar in a mixing bowl. Separately, mix together the egg, milk, oil, vanilla and bananas.

3. Add the wet ingredients to the dry, and mix together until just combined. It does not matter if there are a few lumps of flour in the mixture, and overmixing the batter will make for tough muffins.

4. Divide the mixture between six paper muffin cases in a muffin tin (although I make these in a silicone muffin tin) or arranged snugly in a high-sided baking tin or roasting tray so that the mixture can't make the muffin cases splay out.

5. Spoon a generous dollop of Nutella on top of each muffin and swirl it into the batter. Bake the muffins for 20 minutes until they are puffy and golden. Remove the muffins from the tin so that they cool down enough to eat.

STORECUPBOARD

150g plain flour

1 teaspoon baking powder

a pinch of salt

3 tablespoons golden caster sugar

3½ tablespoons light oil

½ teaspoon vanilla extract

FRESH

1 large egg

3 tablespoons milk

2 ripe bananas, mashed

Nutella, softened in a warm place

RUM-SPIKED BANANA BREAD

SERVES: 6–8 | **PREP TIME:** 15 minutes | **COOKING TIME:** 1 hour 10 minutes

Banana bread is always the answer when you have a couple of bananas going brown hanging around the kitchen. This is what happens when you let me loose on my mother's go-to recipe – I spike it with rum and pack it with chocolate chips.

This is great on the day you make it, and after that toasted and spread with salted butter.

1. Preheat the oven to 180°C/350°F/ Gas mark 4 and line a 900g loaf tin (they make two sizes, you're after the larger one) with a loaf liner or baking parchment.

2. Beat together in a large mixing bowl the butter and the sugar until light and fluffy. Add the eggs one at a time and beat until smooth.

3. Mash the bananas and stir them into the mixture along with the buttermilk and the rum. Mix in the bicarbonate of soda, salt and plain flour until everything is just combined, then fold in the chocolate chips.

4. Pour the mixture into the loaf tin and bake for 1 hour 10 minutes, until the loaf is cracked and golden on top. If you insert a sharp knife or a skewer into the loaf, it should come out clean.

5. Remove the loaf from the tin as soon as it is cool enough to touch, and wait at least half an hour before slicing.

STORECUPBOARD

120g golden caster sugar

1 teaspoon bicarbonate of soda

a pinch of salt

280g plain flour

FRESH

100g unsalted butter, at room temperature

2 large eggs

3 ripe bananas

100ml buttermilk

3 tablespoons rum

75g dark or plain chocolate chips

ONE-BOWL CHOCOLATE CAKE

SERVES: 6–8 | **PREP TIME:** 30 minutes | **COOKING TIME:** 30 minutes

Everyone needs a good chocolate cake in their repertoire. Bake this cake for someone's birthday, when you've got people coming to visit at the weekend or just because.

What people tend to love about this cake is the super-easy yoghurt icing. It adds a nice tang to the cake, and makes it just that little bit more interesting than a regular chocolate sponge. You can use softened butter instead of margarine, but I find that margarine makes for a lighter sponge.

1. Preheat the oven to 180°C/350°F/Gas mark 4. Line the base of a 20cm cake tin with baking parchment and grease the sides with a little margarine.

2. In a mixing bowl using a mixing spoon, beat together the sugar and margarine until light and fluffy. Beat in the vanilla, followed by the eggs, one at a time. Sift in the baking powder, flour and cocoa powder until everything is just combined.

3. Mix in 1 tablespoon of boiling water and pour the cake batter into the prepared tin. Shake the tin a little to help knock out any big air bubbles, and bake in the oven for 20 minutes.

4. The cake should be firm and slightly springy to the touch when it is cooked, and when you insert a sharp knife or a skewer into the middle, it should come out clean. Don't open the oven door to check if the cake is ready until it has been in for at least 25 minutes, otherwise it may sink in the middle.

5. Once the cake is cool enough to touch, transfer it from the tin onto a wire rack to cool. Meanwhile, make the yoghurt icing.

6. Melt the chocolate in an ovenproof bowl in the microwave in 30-second bursts (or melt over a pan of simmering water – see page 150). Once the chocolate is almost entirely melted, stir vigorously to finish the job. Leave it to cool for 5 to 10 minutes. Alternatively, I sometimes use chocolate chips here so I don't need to bother chopping the chocolate.

7. Gently stir in the yoghurt and the honey until the icing is just combined. If you over-stir, it will stiffen too much and become unmanageable. Don't leave out the honey or the icing will be lumpy.

8. Once the cake is cool, smooth the icing over the top, pushing it gently towards the edges so that it just spills over.

STORECUPBOARD

170g golden caster sugar

1 teaspoon vanilla extract

2 teaspoons baking powder

120g plain flour

5 tablespoons cocoa powder

200g plain chocolate, chopped into small pieces

1 tablespoon runny honey

FRESH

170g margarine, plus extra for greasing

3 eggs

100g natural yoghurt

EASY CHOCOLATE BROWNIES

MAKES: 16 brownies | **PREP TIME**: 10 minutes, plus 10 minutes cooling | **COOKING TIME**: 20 minutes

In my second year I stumbled across the idea online to make brownies with cocoa powder, rather than melted chocolate. The first recipe I tried resulted in the easiest, richest brownies I'd ever made. I've worked on simplifying a recipe for these squishy, chocolatey squares down to the bare bones, and this is the result.

One of the earlier versions of these brownies has been the most popular recipe ever on my blog, and they've been baked by blog readers all over the world from Canada to Pakistan. I hope that you enjoy them too.

1. Preheat the oven to 160°C/325°F/Gas mark 3 and line a 24cm square cake tin or brownie pan with foil.

2. Boil a kettle, and pour a few inches of boiling water into a saucepan. Set the saucepan over a very low heat. Measure the butter, sugar, cocoa powder and salt into a heatproof glass bowl and set the bowl over the saucepan of water. The water should not touch the bottom of the bowl, and the steam from the water should melt the butter in the bowl. You can also use this method to melt chocolate.

3. Gradually stir the butter as it melts, until the mixture in the bowl is smooth, and remove from the heat to cool for 10 minutes. You need to let the mixture cool a little, so that the eggs don't instantly cook when you add them.

4. Beat the vanilla extract into the chocolate mixture, followed by the eggs, one by one. Mix in the flour, and pour the batter into the cake tin or brownie pan.

5. Bake the brownie mixture for 20 minutes. Remove from the oven and lift the foil-wrapped giant brownie out of the pan. Leave it to cool before peeling off the foil and slicing it into 16 squares. Store in an airtight container for up to 3 days.

STORECUPBOARD

300g golden caster sugar

100g cocoa powder

¼ teaspoon salt

½ teaspoon vanilla extract

120g plain flour

FRESH

150g unsalted butter

2 large eggs

RAINBOW SPRINKLE RICE KRISPIE TREATS

MAKES: 16 squares | **PREP TIME**: 5 minutes, plus 15 minutes chilling | **COOKING TIME**: 10 minutes

Some people would say that Rice Krispie treats are for kids, and I've added to the kids' birthday party theme by throwing some rainbow sprinkles into the mix. To balance out the extra sugar hit, I've made these gooey squares slightly more grown up by adding in a bit of sea salt. The salty/sweet combination is not for everyone though, so feel free to leave it out.

1. Line a brownie pan (or whatever shallow pan you have that is about 24cm square) with a double layer of cling film.

2. Melt the butter over a medium heat in a large saucepan. Once the butter has melted, stir in the marshmallows until they have melted into the butter to form a goo. Stir in the Rice Krispies until they are well coated in the marshmallow mix. Add the rainbow sprinkles and the salt, and stir until the sprinkles are well distributed. Remove the pan from the heat.

3. Spoon the mixture into the prepared pan and press it in, making sure the mixture reaches every corner. Stash in the fridge for 15 minutes until the mixture has hardened.

4. Tip the pan upside down over a clean chopping board and peel off the cling film. Using a large knife, cut into 16 squares.

5. Store the Rice Krispie treats in an airtight container in a cool place. They should keep for 2 to 3 days, if they even last that long!

STORECUPBOARD

a large pinch of sea salt

FRESH

50g unsalted butter

80g mini white marshmallows

100g Rice Krispies

2 tablespoons rainbow sprinkles

RASPBERRY & LIMONCELLO VICTORIA SANDWICH

SERVES: 6–8 | **PREP TIME:** 30 minutes | **COOKING TIME:** 25 minutes

A classic Victoria sandwich is one of the easiest, but also most impressive, cakes you can bake. While the original is great for afternoon tea, I've jazzed it up a little here with a limoncello buttercream and some fresh raspberries to make it a bit more of a celebration cake, or perfect for dessert.

You can use this recipe to make a classic Victoria sandwich by filling the cake with fresh strawberries and cream with a little icing sugar whipped into it. In our family we like to make a cake that lasts a couple of days by sandwiching it with vanilla buttercream (100g butter to 200g icing sugar, plus 1 teaspoon vanilla extract) and raspberry jam.

While we're on the subject of substitutions, you can use room-temperature butter instead of margarine in the sponge if you'd like. I just find that margarine makes a lighter sponge.

1. Preheat the oven to 180°C/350°F/Gas mark 4 and line the base of a 20cm deep-sided cake tin with baking parchment, buttering the sides with margarine.

2. In a mixing bowl and using a spoon, beat together the sugar and the margarine until light and fluffy. Beat in the eggs, one at a time, followed by the vanilla, until the mixture is smooth. Stir in the salt, baking powder and flour until the mixture is just smooth.

3. Mix in 1 tablespoon boiling water and pour the batter into the cake tin. Bake for 25 minutes until the sponge is springy and golden, and when you insert a sharp knife or a skewer into the middle, it comes out clean.

4. Once the cake is cool enough to touch, turn the cake out onto a wire rack and leave until it is completely cool. In the meantime, make the limoncello buttercream.

5. Beat together the butter and the icing sugar until smooth. Add the limoncello to loosen up the mixture, and then beat in the lemon zest.

6. Once the cake is completely cool, use a very sharp knife (preferably a bread knife) to cut it in half horizontally. Place the bottom half on a serving plate, and top with two-thirds of the buttercream. Spread the remainder of the buttercream over the bottom of the top half of the cake. Scatter raspberries on the bottom half of the cake, and sandwich together with the top half.

STORECUPBOARD

170g golden caster sugar

½ teaspoon vanilla extract

a pinch of salt

1½ teaspoons baking powder

170g plain flour

FRESH

170g margarine, plus extra for greasing

3 large eggs

80g unsalted butter, at room temperature

200g icing sugar

1 tablespoon limoncello

zest of 1 lemon

1 x 150g punnet fresh rasberries

EASY NUTELLA CHEESECAKE CUPS

MAKES: 4 cheesecakes | **PREP TIME**: 10 minutes, plus 2 hours chilling

The combination of Nutella and mascarpone cheese makes for the perfect, simple no-bake cheesecake. If you're making these in winter when Nutella still might be solid at rom temperature, you may need to sit the jar somewhere warm, like on top of a radiator, for half an hour to make sure it is smooth.

1. Put the digestive biscuits in a plastic bag without holes in and tie a knot in the it. Using the end of a rolling pin, empty wine bottle or jar, a tin from the cupboard or even your fist, bash the biscuits until they form crumbs.

2. In a small bowl, melt the butter for a minute in the microwave or in a small saucepan over a low heat. Add the biscuit crumbs to the melted butter with the sea salt and mix until everything is combined. Divide the crumbs between four ramekins or small glasses and press into the corners with your fingers to create a firm biscuit base.

3. Beat together the mascarpone and Nutella until smooth, and divide between the four ramekins. Smooth over the top of each of the cheesecake cups, and transfer to the fridge to chill and firm up for a couple of hours.

STORECUPBOARD

a generous pinch of sea salt

FRESH

4 digestive biscuits

30g unsalted butter

1 x 250g tub light mascarpone, at room temperature

120g Nutella, at room temperature

LIME CHEESECAKE CUPS

MAKES: 4 cheesecakes | **PREP TIME**: 15 minutes, plus 1 hour chilling

These easy zesty, creamy cheesecake cups would be perfect to finish off a Mexican meal. I like to serve them up for dessert after I've made a big stack of Chicken Fajitas (page 126) with all of the accompaniments and a couple of beer margaritas (page 174) for friends on a Saturday night.

Usually I don't mind if I use full-fat mascarpone or light mascarpone in desserts, but here light mascarpone is best as it makes for a smoother cheesecake once combined with the lime, as the citrus juice sets the cheesecake.

1. Melt the butter in the microwave or in a small saucepan over a low heat and add the salt. Place the biscuits in a plastic bag, tie a knot in the top and bash the bag with a rolling pin or another heavy object to create crumbs. Mix the butter and the crumbs together to create the biscuit base. Divide the base between four ramekins or small glasses and, using your fingertips, press the biscuit crumbs down to create a solid base.

2. Beat together the mascarpone, icing sugar, lime zest and juice until smooth. Divide the mixture between the four ramekins and smooth it into the corners with the back of a teaspoon.

3. Chill in the fridge for at least an hour until the cheesecakes have had a chance to set. Sprinkle the top of each cheesecake with a little more lime zest, if you have any, before serving.

STORECUPBOARD

a pinch of salt

FRESH

30g unsalted butter

4 digestive biscuits

1 x 250g tub light mascarpone, at room temperature

4 teaspoons icing sugar

zest and juice of 1 lime, plus extra zest to decorate (optional)

THAI FRIED BANANAS

SERVES: 1 | **PREP TIME:** 2 minutes | **COOKING TIME:** 3 minutes

This easy Thai-inspired dessert only takes 5 minutes to make, and is the perfect way to finish up any Asian-style meal, especially if you have people over. It is really simple to double or quadruple up to feed more people; just cook the bananas in a bigger pan.

I like these plain, but they're also great served with single cream or a scoop of vanilla or coconut ice cream.

I. Heat the butter in a small frying pan over a medium heat until frothy. Add the banana, followed by the honey and half the lime juice. Fry the banana until all of the liquid has evaporated, then add the coconut. Toss the banana so it is well coated in the coconut, and transfer to a warm bowl. Add the rest of the lime juice, and sprinkle with black sesame seeds, if you have any. Eat straight away.

STORECUPBOARD

I tablespoon runny honey

FRESH

a large knob of butter

I banana, peeled and sliced into chunks on the diagonal

juice of ½ lime

I tablespoon shredded or desiccated coconut

black sesame seeds (optional)

ROCKY ROAD ICE CREAM TERRINE

SERVES: 8 | **PREP TIME:** 15 minutes, plus 2–4 hours freezing

This makes a fantastic dinner party dessert. I like to make it to keep in the freezer so that I can cut off a slice or eight whenever I need an impressive last-minute dessert, but have not had time to make anything.

Use chocolate ice cream to make a classic rocky road. However, for somethig a bit different I like to use salted caramel chocolate ice cream. You don't usually find salted caramel in rocky road, but once you've tried it, you'll think all rocky road needs it.

1. Take the ice cream out of the freezer so it starts to soften. Double-line a 900g loaf tin (they typically make two sizes of loaf tin; you want the biggest) with cling film, with enough to drape over the sides of the tin. Break up the biscuits into small chunks. Rinse the cherries and quarter them.

2. Scoop the ice cream into a large bowl and add the biscuit and cherry pieces, along with the marshmallows and sultanas. With a mixing spoon, mash all of the ingredients together until they are combined, but the ice cream is still at least partly frozen. Press the mixture into the loaf tin, fold the overhanging cling film over the top and refreeze for 2 to 4 hours until the ice cream is solid again.

3. Take the ice cream terrine out of the freezer 5 to 10 minutes before you want to slice it.

FRESH

1 x 500g tub chocolate ice cream

6 digestive biscuits

100g glacé cherries (approximately 2 handfuls)

50g mini marshmallows (approximately 1 large handful)

50g sultanas

CHOCOLATE GANACHE & FRESH RASPBERRY TART

SERVES: 6–8 | **PREP TIME:** 5 minutes, plus 2 hours chilling | **COOKING TIME:** 5 minutes

This easy, four-ingredient tart looks super-impressive, tastes fantastic and requires very little effort at all. Feel free to mix up the fruit a little; I happen to find the combination of raspberries and chocolate ganache irresistible.

1. Gently heat the cream in a small saucepan over a medium-high heat until it is just boiling. Immediately remove it from the heat, and stir in the chocolate chips until they have melted and the chocolate ganache is smooth and uniform. You can use any plain chocolate rather than chocolate chips; just chop it into very small pieces first.

2. Pour the chocolate ganache into the pastry case, and arrange the raspberries in the chocolate. Chill in the fridge for at least 2 hours until the ganache sets and can be sliced. Try to remove it from the fridge about half an hour before serving to take the chill off of the raspberries.

FRESH

1 x 20cm all-butter pastry case

1 x 150ml pot double cream

100g plain chocolate chips

200g fresh raspberries (approximately 2 large handfuls)

CLASSIC CRÊPES WITH SUGAR & SALTED BUTTER

MAKES: 5–6 pancakes | **PREP TIME:** 5 minutes | **COOKING TIME:** 20–25 minutes

I know someone who constantly has a recipe for crepes open on their tablet for weekend mornings. Everyone needs a good recipe for crêpes to hand that will suit any occasion. This recipe serves one, but is easily doubled, tripled or quadrupled.

I always thought that sugar and fresh lemon juice was the ultimate crêpe topping until I had sugar and salted butter as part of a set menu on holiday with my parents. I promise you that it will change your pancake game forever.

1. Melt a small knob of butter in the microwave or in a small pan over a low heat. In a jug, whisk together the egg, milk and melted butter. Gradually add the flour, whisking it in until you have a smooth batter.

2. Heat a small (preferably non-stick) frying pan over a medium-high heat, and melt a little more butter in the pan so that the crêpes don't stick. Once the butter is frothy, pour a little of the batter into the pan and swill it around quickly so that the base of the pan is covered. Cook the crêpe until it starts to curl up at the sides and bubble up in the middle. Flip the pancake, and cook until it is golden on both sides. Transfer to a warm plate while you cook the rest of the pancakes.

3. Melt another knob of butter either in a small saucepan or in the microwave, and stir in a good pinch of sea salt. Serve this over the crêpes as you would a pancake syrup, with a good sprinkling of sugar.

STORECUPBOARD

4 tablespoons plain flour

sea salt

golden caster sugar, to serve

FRESH

unsalted butter

1 large egg

125ml milk

MIXED BERRY & OAT CRUMBLE

SERVES: 4–6 | **PREP TIME:** 10 minutes | **COOKING TIME:** 25–30 minutes

Crumbles are among the most satisfying and easy desserts to make if you want to feed a crowd, or to use up any fruit you may have left over from other recipes. Use this recipe, or my recipe for Rhubarb, Orange & Ginger Crumble (opposite), as a guide for how to turn practically any fruit into a crumble with the topping of your choice. As a general rule of thumb, soft fruits don't need precooking and other fruits do.

If you don't have any ground almonds, just replace with 30g more plain flour.

1. Preheat the oven to 180°C/350°F/Gas mark 4.

2. Peel, core and thinly slice the apple and mix it with the berries and 1 teaspoon sugar. Spoon into the bottom of an ovenproof dish.

3. Mix together the flour, ground almonds and a pinch of salt. Cube the fridge-cold butter and add to the flour mixture. Using your fingertips, rub the flour mixture and the butter together. The mixture should start to form crumbs. Now add the remaining sugar and the oats, and rub them in until everything is combined.

4. Sprinkle the mixture over the berries and bake in the oven for 25 to 30 minutes until the topping is golden and the fruit has started to bubble up from underneath. Serve with vanilla ice cream, Greek yoghurt, crème fraîche or whatever else you have to hand.

STORECUPBOARD

50g golden caster sugar, plus 1 teaspoon for the filling

100g plain flour

a pinch of salt

FRESH

1 eating apple

300g frozen mixed berries, defrosted

50g ground almonds (optional)

75g unsalted butter, cold from the fridge

50g porridge oats

RHUBARB, ORANGE & GINGER CRUMBLE

SERVES: 4–6 | PREP TIME: 10 minutes | COOKING TIME: 35 minutes

While I've already laid out the blueprint for a basic crumble, I wanted to include this version made with rhubarb, orange and a generous amount of ground ginger, as it is just such a great combination. Cosy and warming, this would be perfect served up after a Sunday roast, with single cream, ice cream or even a dollop of thick, rich clotted cream to finish off the meal in style.

Brilliantly pink forced rhubarb or ruby-tinged green English rhubarb work equally well here. For the orange juice you can use either freshly squeezed or from a bottle or carton.

1. Preheat the oven to 200°C/400°F/Gas mark 6.

2. Chop the rhubarb into bite-sized chunks. Arrange the chunks in the bottom of an ovenproof dish and sprinkle over the orange juice and brown sugar. Cover the top of the dish with foil and roast in the oven for 20 minutes until the rhubarb is tender.

3. Meanwhile, make the ginger crumble topping. Combine the flour and the ginger in a mixing bowl. Cut the cold butter into small chunks and add them to the flour mixture. Using your fingertips, rub the flour mixture and the butter together. The mixture should start to form into crumbs. Add the sugar, and rub in until the crumble comes together.

4. Remove the foil from the rhubarb, and sprinkle over the crumble topping. Return to the oven to bake for 15 minutes until the crumble is crisp and golden.

STORECUPBOARD

170g plain flour

55g golden caster sugar

FRESH

2–3 large stalks of rhubarb

1 tablespoon orange juice

1 tablespoon soft light brown sugar

2 teaspoons ground ginger

100g unsalted butter, cold from the fridge

DARK CHOCOLATE & BROWN BREAD & BUTTER PUDDING

SERVES: 3–4 | **PREP TIME:** 10 minutes | **COOKING TIME:** 35–40 minutes

This is my favourite bread and butter pudding. Just as easy, but so much more complex than the regular version, it can be made in one dish or in individual portions. Feel free to adapt this recipe to make a regular bread and butter pudding, forgetting the marmalade, using white bread and switching out the chocolate chips for raisins or currants, and perhaps a little bit of candied peel.

You'll want to use granary bread rather than wholemeal here. When I've tried using wholemeal, the results ended up reminding me far too much of school lunches. If you can't find any, just use white instead. Thick-cut marmalade is best here, but smooth also works if that is all you've got. Demerara sugar makes a lovely, crunchy topping if you've got it, but caster sugar will also work.

1. Preheat the oven to 150°C/300°F/Gas mark 2.

2. Grease an ovenproof dish with butter. Butter one side of each of the pieces of bread. Tear the buttered bread into medium chunks and spread a layer, butter side up, across the bottom of the dish. Sprinkle evenly with half the chocolate chips and spoonfuls of marmalade. Layer with more bread, the rest of the chocolate and some more marmalade. Layer the rest of the bread over the top.

3. To make the custard, place the egg yolks in the bottom of a jug. In a small saucepan, mix together the caster sugar, milk and vanilla and set over a medium-high heat. Whisk until all of the sugar is dissolved and the milk is just boiling. Remove from the heat and gradually mix into the yolks, whisking vigorously.

4. Pour the custard mixture evenly over the bread and buter pudding and sprinkle the top with the demerara sugar. Bake in the oven for 30 minutes until the pudding is set, has puffed up a little and started to brown.

5. Ten minutes before the pudding is due to come out of the oven, preheat the grill to 200°C/400°F. Once the pudding is baked, pop it under the grill for a few minutes until the top is crisp and golden.

STORECUPBOARD

5 teaspoons golden caster sugar

1 teaspoon vanilla extract

FRESH

unsalted butter, at room temperature

5 slices of granary bread

a handful of dark chocolate chips

marmalade

3 large egg yolks

250ml milk

2 tablespoons demerara sugar

WHITE WINE-SOAKED STRAWBERRIES

SERVES: 4 | **PREP TIME:** 5 minutes, plus 4 hours chilling

This is a super-simple and refreshing dessert for the summer. Serve in wine glasses or tumblers with a scoop of vanilla ice cream, over Greek yoghurt or spooned with a bit of cream next to a slice of my One-Bowl Chocolate Cake (page 148).

You want to choose either a fruity white wine here, or something medium and Spanish. Get whatever is on special offer.

1. Hull and thickly slice the strawberries. Place in a small bowl and combine with the sugar, wine and a generous few grinds of black pepper.

2. Leave to chill in the fridge for at least 4 hours before serving. If you can, take the strawberries out of the fridge and bring them up to room temperature beforehand.

STORECUPBOARD

1 teaspoon golden caster sugar

freshly ground black pepper

FRESH

10 large strawberries

100ml white wine

LEMON POSSET

MAKES: 4 pots | **PREP TIME:** 5 minutes, plus 4 hours chilling | **COOKING TIME:** 5 minutes

This lemon posset is super-rich, super-creamy and super-simple. Serve it with fresh berries or just by itself to round off a special meal for friends, or for your family if you've got them coming to visit and you want to show off the culinary skills you've built up since moving out. You don't actually have to tell them how easy it was to make! The lemon and lime juice will react with the cream to make it set, just like magic.

1. Heat the cream and the sugar together in a small saucepan over a medium-high heat, stirring until the sugar has all dissolved and the cream is just starting to boil. Remove the pan from the heat and stir in the lemon and lime juice.

2. Divide the cream between four small pots or wine glasses, and leave to set in the fridge for at least 4 hours. Decorate with curls of lemon zest before serving.

STORECUPBOARD

75g golden caster sugar

FRESH

1 x 300ml pot double cream

juice of ½ lemon

juice of ¼ lime

curls of lemon zest, to decorate

BOOZY SMOOTHIE ICE LOLLIES

MAKES: 10 lollies | **PREP TIME**: 10 minutes, plus 5–6 hours freezing

You can save old yoghurt pots to make ice lollies in, but if you're a popsicle person I'd invest in some cheap lolly moulds as you can freeze anything from fruit juice to yoghurt to make frozen desserts and snacks. Typically, you can pretty much make any grown-up, boozy smoothie combination by mixing a carton of smoothie with 85g alcohol. My favourite combinations are strawberry and banana smoothie mixed with limoncello, as here, and piña colada lollies made with coconut, pineapple and banana smoothie and rum.

Alcohol does not freeze, so too much booze may stop the lollies from freezing. You'll be okay with any spirit containing 40% alcohol or less. Vodka is typically around 40%.

1. Combine the smoothie and the limoncello, and pour into 10 lolly moulds. Freeze for at least 5 to 6 hours, before removing the lollies and wrapping them individually in cling film for freezer storage.

2. If you're making the lollies in yoghurt pots, freeze them for an hour before inserting a wooden lolly stick in each so that it stands up straight.

FRESH

1 x 750ml carton strawberry and banana smoothie

85ml limoncello

DRINKS

COCONUT HOT CHOCOLATE

MAKES: 1 mug | **PREP TIME**: 5 minutes | **COOKING TIME**: 5 minutes

This is a great way to use up the end of a tin of coconut milk you've opened to make soup or a curry, with the added bonus that this rich and creamy hot chocolate is perfect for people who are lactose intolerant. Any type of coconut milk will do, though you might want to add a little less water if you're using the stuff that comes in a carton. Also, you might want to add a little more or a little less sugar depending on how sweet you like it. Serve with mini marshmallows, if liked.

1. Combine all of the ingredients with 150ml water in a small saucepan and whisk over a medium-high heat until the hot chocolate is smooth and piping hot.

STORECUPBOARD

1½ tablespoons cocoa powder

1½ teaspoons golden caster sugar

½ teaspoon vanilla extract

FRESH

100ml coconut milk

mini marshmallows, to serve

EARL GREY ICED TEA

MAKES: 4 glasses | **PREP TIME**: 5 minutes, plus 5–6 hours chilling | **COOKING TIME**: 4 minutes

I honestly do not understand why in England, this great tea-drinking country, we don't have a tradition of serving up pitchers of iced tea during the summer months. So I've created an 'English' version of the all-American classic, using delicately floral Earl Grey tea bags.

It turns out that Earl Grey also makes a rather delicious hot, sweet tea, too. Just stir 50g of golden caster sugar into the boiling water before brewing the tea.

1. Pour 1 litre boiling water over the tea bags in a large jug and allow to brew for 4 minutes. Allow to cool, then chill in the fridge for around 6 hours, and serve over ice with a thick slice of lemon.

FRESH

5 Earl Grey tea bags

a small handful of ice cubes

a thick slice of lemon, to serve

THYME LEMONADE

MAKES: 4 big glasses | **PREP TIME:** 10 minutes, plus 3–4 hours cooling

I prefer to cook with fresh herbs, but that sometimes means a lot of leftovers in the bottom of my fridge. I find leftover woody herbs make simply delicious infused lemonades, which double as great alternatives to fizzy drinks. To make rosemary lemonade, replace the 6 sprigs of fresh thyme with 3 sprigs of fresh rosemary. If you happen to have lavender bushes growing near you, use 6 fresh lavender heads instead. Obviously, you can also use this recipe to make classic lemonade, leaving out the herbs altogether.

While I usually use golden caster sugar for everything, white caster sugar here provides a much cleaner and more classic taste. However, golden caster sugar will work perfectly well, adding a pleasant hint of caramel to your lemonade.

FRESH

75g white caster sugar

6 large sprigs of fresh thyme

4 large lemons

1. Combine 250ml boiling water with the sugar in a medium or large saucepan. Over a medium heat, stir until all of the sugar has dissolved. Remove the pan from the heat to cool.

2. Add the thyme sprigs to 750ml boiling water and leave to steep while you squeeze the lemons.

3. Add the lemon juice to the syrup. Remove the thyme sprigs from the steeping water, and add the lemonade mixture.

4. Leave to cool completely before refrigerating in a clean sealed jar or bottle for up to 2 days.

CLASSIC MARGARITA

MAKES: I glass | **PREP TIME:** 5 minutes

Margaritas are the perfect accompaniment to any type of Mexican food, or indeed anything at all. It is totally up to you if you serve these neat or over ice. You can use any type of tequila to make margaritas, but I prefer to use white tequila as I find it has a fresher, cleaner taste.

To make a pair of beer margaritas, double this recipe and mix the shaken cocktail with a 330ml bottle of light Mexican beer.

1. Combine the lime juice, tequila and triple sec with a handful of ice cubes in a cocktail shaker or a jam jar with a lid. Shake well, and drain into a glass rimmed with sea salt. You can do this by first dipping the rim of the glass in water, then a dish of sea salt. Garnish with lime slices.

STORECUPBOARD

fine sea salt

FRESH

juice of I lime (30ml), plus lime slices to garnish

30ml tequila

20ml triple sec

a small handful of ice cubes

BROWN SUGAR MOJITO

MAKES: 1 glass | **PREP TIME**: 5 minutes

Two of my closest friends are known for their love of mojitos: Kathryn for making them, and Sherin for drinking them! So, I simply had to come up with an easy mojito recipe that anyone (even Sherin, who is a disaster in the kitchen) can put together.

To make an easy raspberry mojito, press 100g (or a very large handful) of fresh raspberries through a sieve to make a seedless raspberry purée. Muddle this in with the sugar and mint leaves.

1. Cut the limes into small wedges. In the bottom of a large glass, muddle together the limes, mint leaves and sugar with the end of a rolling pin or a large spoon. You're aiming for the mint leaves to be slightly bruised (but not overly so), and for the juice to have started to come out of the lime wedges. Pour over the rum.

2. Add the ice cubes, and pour everything into another glass. Fill the glass to the top with soda water. Garnish with another mint sprig and a straw.

FRESH

1½ limes

leaves of 2–3 fresh mint sprigs, plus an extra sprig to garnish

2 teaspoons soft light brown sugar

60ml white rum

a handful of ice cubes

90ml soda water

CLASSIC SANGRIA

SERVES: 4 | **PREP TIME**: 10 minutes, plus 4 hours chilling

Otherwise known as a Spanish summer's day. Really, you can add whatever fruit you want, and if you don't have any brandy but you do have dark rum, you can use that instead, with good results.

While the sangria will improve during chilling as the flavours from the fruit infuse into the wine, you can make up a jug at short notice by keeping a bottle of red wine and the lemonade in the fridge ready to mix.

1. Add all of the fruit to the bottom of a large jug.

2. Add the wine, brandy, triple sec and lemonade. Stir everything well, and taste. Depending on the brand of lemonade you've used and the type of wine, it might be sweet enough already. If you think it needs a bit of sugar, stir in the teaspoon of golden caster sugar until it has all dissolved.

3. Chill for at least 4 hours, and then serve in highball glasses or the largest wine glasses you have.

STORECUPBOARD

1 teaspoon golden caster sugar (optional)

FRESH

1 small apple, cored and cubed

a handful of strawberries, hulled

¼ orange, sliced

1 bottle of red wine

60ml brandy

60ml triple sec

100ml sparkling lemonade

MULLED WINE

SERVES: 4 | **PREP TIME**: 5 minutes | **COOKING TIME**: 20 minutes

You know winter is coming when food markets start to sell fragrant, steaming mugs of mulled wine, perfectly disguised for sneaking back to the library with you.

You want to use a carton of fresh orange juice from the refrigerator section here, rather than the juice of fresh oranges or the stuff you buy to keep in the kitchen cupboard.

1. Using a skewer or another sharp object, prick the clementine all the way around horizontally, then vertically, as if you were creating a cross all the way around the fruit. Push cloves into the holes.

2. Combine the wine, orange juice, 100ml water and the sugar in a lidded saucepan. Add the clove-studded clementine, the star anise and the cinnamon stick. Set over a low heat, and stir until the sugar has dissolved.

3. Reduce the heat to the lowest it will go, and put the lid on the saucepan. Leave to simmer for 15 minutes. Add the brandy, and strain the mulled wine through a sieve to remove any broken pieces of cinnamon before serving.

STORECUPBOARD

4 tablespoons golden caster sugar

FRESH

1 clementine

cloves

1 bottle of red wine

200ml orange juice

1 star anise

½ cinnamon stick

1 tablespoon brandy

MEAL MATHS

When I go shopping, I like to pick up a few items that can be used to make a couple of meals, both so that I'm sorted for a few days and so that I cut down on as much food waste as possible from half-used packets of things.

Here are some easy meal formulas that I hope will give you a few ideas of which recipes you can shop for all in one go. **Take One Recipe** contains suggestions for how leftovers from one meal can be reused in others, my formulas for **Using Everything Up** should help you cut down on waste, while **Storecupboard Meals** suggest dishes you can make when you have not had time to go shopping.

There are also ideas for casual meals in **Food for Friends** and some memorable menus in **Special Occasions**. Lastly, **Three Meals for under £10** hopes to give you a little bit of inspiration for those times when your money has almost run out!

TAKE ONE RECIPE

1
Chorizo Baked Beans (page 24) **on toast = Baked Egg & Homemade Baked Bean Pots** (page 32) **+ a fantastic side for a full English breakfast**

STORECUPBOARD

dried oregano
Worcestershire sauce
Dijon mustard
balsamic vinegar
golden caster sugar
light oil
½ chicken stock cube
I small onion
2 large garlic cloves
2 x 400g tins chopped
 tomatoes
sea salt and black
 pepper

FRESH

8cm eating chorizo
2 x 400g tins cannellini
 beans
6 large eggs
bread, for toasting
sausages
bacon
tomatoes

Chorizo Baked Beans (page 24)

2
Chicken Fajitas (page 126) **= Leftover Fajita Burritos** (page 72) **+ California Scrambled Eggs** (page 34)

STORECUPBOARD

3 white onions
I red onion
brown rice
dried oregano
light oil
chilli powder
ground cumin
sea salt

FRESH

2 limes
sweet smoked paprika
cayenne pepper
2 large chicken breasts
I red pepper
I yellow pepper

tequila
10 tortilla wraps
2 large tomatoes
I jalapeño pepper
I large pack fresh
 coriander
3 large ripe avocados
I medium pot soured
 cream
5 large eggs
bread, for toasting
unsalted butter

OR A Loaded Fajita Salad (page 69) **+ Hangover-Cure Mexican Chilaquiles** (page 43)

STORECUPBOARD

3 white onions
I red onion
dried oregano
light oil
chilli powder
ground cumin
sea salt

FRESH

3 limes
sweet smoked paprika
cayenne pepper
2 large chicken breasts
I red pepper
I yellow pepper
tequila

10 tortilla wraps
2 large tomatoes
I jalapeño pepper
I large pack fresh
 coriander
3 large ripe avocados
I medium pot soured
 cream
I large radish
I x 400g tin kidney beans
I x 400g tin black beans
I large egg
I small pack salad leaves

3 Easy Lemon & Thyme Roast Chicken with Za'atar Potatoes (page 138) + a salad or vegetables = Leftover Roast Chicken Pie (page 140)

STORECUPBOARD	FRESH
plain flour	1 large chicken
1 chicken stock cube	unsalted butter
light oil	1 small pack fresh thyme
sea salt and black	1 lemon
pepper	1 x 500g pack new
	potatoes
	za'atar
	salad or vegetables
	2 leeks
	1 pack mushrooms
	1 pack bacon
	1 x 150ml pot single
	cream
	1 x 375g block puff pastry
	milk

OR Warm Leftover Roast Chicken Honey Mustard Pasta Salad (page 52) + Leftover Roast Chicken, Pesto Mayo & Tomato Sandwich (page 62)

STORECUPBOARD	FRESH
light oil	1 large chicken
light mayonnaise	unsalted butter
pesto	1 small pack fresh thyme
1 pack pasta shapes	1 lemon
wholegrain mustard	1 x 500g pack new
runny honey	potatoes
extra virgin olive oil	za'atar
white wine vinegar	salad or vegetables
sea salt and black	1 small pack cherry
pepper	tomatoes
	1 small pack rocket
	1 large tomato
	bread, for slicing

4 Spiced Lamb Patties with Light Tzatziki & Pitta Bread (page 131) = Light Tzatziki with Home-Baked Pitta Chips (page 78) + Fattoush (page 75)

STORECUPBOARD	FRESH
2 red onions	1 x 500g pack lamb mince
1 garlic clove	1 small pack fresh mint
extra virgin olive oil	1 lemon
ground cumin	2 packs pittas
sea salt and black	1 small pack salad
pepper	2 cucumbers
	1 small pack fresh dill
	1 x 500g tub light Greek
	yoghurt
	sumac or za'atar
	6 radishes
	1 large pack cherry
	tomatoes
	1 Little Gem lettuce
	1 small pack fresh
	parsley

5 Sausage Bolognese (page 134) = Frying-Pan Lasagne (page 95) + cheesy twice-cooked bolognese baked potato (page 105)

STORECUPBOARD	FRESH
1 white onion	1 large carrot
2 garlic cloves	1 celery stick
1 x 400g tin chopped	1 x 450g pack sausage
tomatoes	meat
dried oregano	1 bottle red wine
golden caster sugar	tomato purée
1 chicken or beef stock	6 dried lasagne sheets
cube	2 mozzarella balls
light oil	1 baking potato
sea salt and black	grated cheese
pepper	

Fattoush (page 75)

SPECIAL OCCASIONS

1 DINNER FOR TWO = Sharing Steak with Thyme-Roasted Cherry Tomatoes (page 116) **+ White Wine-Soaked Strawberries** (page 164) **+ the rest of the bottle of wine**

STORECUPBOARD

golden caster sugar
balsamic vinegar
extra virgin olive oil
light oil
sea salt and black
   pepper

FRESH

1 large pack cherry
   tomatoes
1 punnet strawberries
1 small pack fresh thyme
1 large steak
1 bottle white wine

2 SUNDAY LUNCH FOR TWO = One-Pan Chicken Roast with Root Vegetables (page 124) **+ Lemon Posset** (page 165) **+ a bottle of white wine or Prosecco**

STORECUPBOARD

2 red onions
4 garlic cloves
light oil
golden caster sugar
sea salt and black
   pepper

FRESH

1 butternut squash
1 sweet potato
2 parsnips
2 carrots
4 skin-on, bone-in
   chicken thighs
1 x 300ml pot double
   cream
1 lemon
1 lime
1 bottle white wine
   or Prosecco

3 SUNDAY LUNCH FOR A CROWD = Easy Lemon & Thyme Roast Chicken with Za'atar Potatoes (page 138) **+ green salad + Dark Chocolate & Brown Bread & Butter Pudding** (page 162)

STORECUPBOARD

vanilla extract
golden caster sugar
light oil
sea salt and black
   pepper

FRESH

1 large chicken
unsalted butter
1 small pack fresh thyme
1 lemon
1 x 500g pack new
   potatoes
za'atar
2 large bags salad leaves
sliced granary bread
dark chocolate chips
marmalade
3 large eggs
1 pint milk
demerara sugar

4 GRADUATION BRUNCH = Full English Breakfast Quiche (page 46) **+ a green salad + Cheat's Vegetable Juice Bloody Mary** (page 42)

STORECUPBOARD

Tabasco
Worcestershire sauce
sea salt and black
   pepper

FRESH

1 pack sausages
1 pack streaky bacon
1 pack chestnut
   mushrooms
4 large eggs
1 x 150ml tub single
   cream
1 pint milk
unsalted butter
1 large pack cherry
   tomatoes
1 lemon
1 x 320g shortcrust
   pastry sheet
2 cartons vegetable juice
vodka
1 large bag salad leaves
1 pack leafy celery

THREE MEALS FOR UNDER £10

 1 Dippy Eggs with Anchovy Butter Soldiers (page 35) + **Easy Smoked Mackerel Pâté** (page 81) + **Grated Courgette Pasta** (page 88)

STORECUPBOARD

anchovy fillets in olive oil
nonpareille capers
1 pack pasta shapes
extra virgin olive oil
sea salt and black pepper

FRESH

2 large eggs
bread, for toasting
unsalted butter
1 x small tub light Greek yoghurt
1 lemon
1 red chilli (fresh or dried)
1 courgette
1 tin smoked mackerel

 2 Chicken Livers & Onions on Toast (page 30) + **Israeli Chopped Mixed Bean Salad** (page 59) + **Tuna & Pesto Rice** (page 99)

STORECUPBOARD

1 large white onion
brown rice
pesto
extra virgin olive oil
sea salt and black pepper

FRESH

unsalted butter
1 pack chicken livers
bread, for toasting
1 cucumber
1 bunch spring onions
2 large tomatoes
1 small pack flat-leaf parsley
1 lemon
za'atar
1 tin tuna
1 x 400g tin mixed beans

 3 Ten-Minute Mushrooms & Bacon on Toast (page 85) + **Devilled Egg Sandwich** (page 64) + **inned Tomato Pasta Sauce** (page 89)

STORECUPBOARD

dried oregano
light mayonnaise
Dijon mustard
Tabasco
1 x 400g tin chopped tomatoes
1 pack pasta shapes
sea salt and black pepper

FRESH

bread, for slicing
unsalted butter
2 large eggs
1 bunch spring onions
1 pack chestnut mushrooms
1 pack streaky bacon
1 small pack fresh parsley
1 small pack salad leaves
soft light brown sugar

4 Honeyed Cardamom-Soaked Apricots with Pistachios & Greek Yoghurt (page 23) + **Roast Bone Marrow with Gremolata** (page 82) + **Indian Spiced Potatoes** (page 83) **with yoghurt and chutney**

STORECUPBOARD

runny honey
ground cumin
chilli powder
1 garlic clove
light oil
sea salt and black pepper

FRESH

dried apricots
green cardamom pods
1 orange
1 lemon
1 large baking potato
1 large pot Greek yoghurt
mango chutney
ground coriander
ground turmeric
shelled pistachios
1 piece of bonemarrow, halved lengthways
bread, for slicing
1 small pack fresh parsley

A

anchovy 92
chicken schnitzel with capers, anchovies & a fried egg 108–9
dippy eggs with anchovy butter soldiers 35, 187
roasted red peppers with tomatoes & anchovies 118
apricot, honeyed cardamom-soaked apricots with pistachios & Greek yoghurt 23
avocado 34, 43, 126–7
bacon & avocado wraps with skinny buttermilk ranch dressing 67
BLTA chopped salad with skinny buttermilk ranch dressing 60, 182
hot salmon & avocado salad with soured cream & lime dressing 61

B

bacon 46–7, 140–1
bacon & avocado wraps with skinny buttermilk ranch dressing 67, 182
bacon & bean hot pot 133
BLTA chopped salad with skinny buttermilk ranch dressing 60, 182
ten-minute mushrooms & bacon on toast 85, 187
bagels
pesto, ricotta & Parma ham bagel pizzas 79
smoked salmon bagel breakfast casserole 26–7
banana
autumn-spiced banana pancakes 37
banana & Nutella muffins 146
rum-spiked banana bread 147
Thai fried banana 156
bean(s) 43
bacon & bean hot pot 133
baked egg & homemade baked bean pots 32, 179
chorizo baked beans 24–5, 32, 179
Israeli chopped mixed bean salad 59, 187
super-easy meat-free mixed bean chilli 132
berries 39
granola, spinach, yoghurt & berries 20–1
mixed berry & oat crumble 160
see also blueberry; raspberry; strawberry
bloody Mary, cheat's vegetable juice 42, 186
blueberry & oat breakfast muffins 39
bolognese, sausage 95, 134–5, 137, 180, 184
bone marrow, roast, with gremolata 82, 187
bread 34, 63, 75, 82, 123
classic savoury eggy bread 29, 182
dark chocolate & brown bread-&-butter pudding 162–3, 186
leftover bread panzanella salad 73, 182
rum-spiked banana bread 147
see also pitta bread; sandwiches; toast
brownies, easy chocolate 150
burritos, leftover fajita 72, 179
butter, anchovy 35
buttermilk 37, 39
overnight buttermilk pancakes 36, 182
skinny buttermilk ranch dressing 60, 67

C

cakes
one-bowl chocolate 148–9, 184
raspberry & limoncello Victoria sandwich 152–3
see also brownies; muffins
carrot 53, 66, 97, 124, 133, 134
carrot soup 96
casserole, smoked salmon bagel breakfast 26–7
cheesecake
easy Nutella cheesecake cups 154, 185
lime cheesecake cups 155, 185
chicken
a basic chicken soup 97
chicken fajitas with salsa & boozy guacamole 69, 72, 126–7, 179, 185
chicken noodle & oyster sauce stir-fry 113
chicken schnitzel with capers, anchovies & a fried egg 108–9
easy lemon & thyme roast chicken with za'atar potatoes 138–9, 180, 186
leftover roast chicken, pesto mayo & tomato sandwich 62, 180
leftover roast chicken pie 140–1, 180
one-pan chicken roast with root vegetables 124, 186
one-pan chicken roast with summer vegetables 125
slightly sticky & slightly spicy chicken wings 74
warm leftover roast chicken honey mustard pasta salad 52, 180
chicken liver & onions on toast 30, 187
chilaquiles, hangover-cure 43, 179
chilli, super-easy meat-free mixed bean 132, 185
chocolate 15, 144, 147
chocolate ganache & fresh raspberry tart 158
coconut hot chocolate 170, 182
dark chocolate & brown bread-&-butter pudding 162–3, 186
easy chocolate brownies 150
one-bowl chocolate cake 148–9, 184
orange chocolate chip cookies 145
chorizo baked beans 24–5, 32, 179
coconut 20, 128, 156
coconut hot chocolate 170
quick & creamy pumpkin & coconut soup 98
compote, forced rhubarb & cardamom breakfast 22
cookies, orange chocolate chip 145
courgette 76, 93, 125
grated courgette pasta 88, 187
couscous, good green 51
crème fraîche, lemon 44–5
crepes, classic crepes with salted butter & sugar 159
crumble
mixed berry & oat 160
rhubarb, orange & ginger 161
cucumber 51, 54, 59, 65, 66, 75, 78
mackerel mayo & quick pickled cucumber sandwiches 65
curry, easy root veg 128–9, 182, 184

D

dressings
skinny buttermilk ranch 60, 67
soured cream & lime 69

E

Earl Grey iced tea 171
egg 43, 46–7, 112
baked egg & homemade baked
bean pots 32, 179
California scrambled eggs 34, 179
chicken schnitzel with capers,
anchovies & a fried egg 108–9
classic savoury eggy bread 29, 182
devilled egg sandwich 64, 187
dippy eggs with anchovy butter
soldiers 35, 187
gammon & egg with Cajun potato
wedges 106–7
green eggs & ham 33
leftover baked Indian-spiced
potatoes with tomato, egg &
coriander 28
pea, prawn & mushroom egg fried
rice 111
single-serving spicy baked eggs in
tomato sauce 31

F

fajitas
chicken fajitas with salsa & boozy
guacamole 69, 72, 126–7, 179, 185
leftover fajita burritos 72, 179
loaded fajita salad with soured
cream & lime dressing 69, 179
fattoush 75, 180–1
fish
kitchen cupboard fishcakes 102–3
see also mackerel; salmon; tuna
fritters, Indian spiced leftover
summer vegetable 76–7

G

gammon & egg with Cajun potato
wedges 106–7
ganache, chocolate ganache & fresh
raspberry tart 158
ginger, rhubarb & orange crumble 161

granola with spinach, yoghurt &
berries 20–1
gravy, onion 120–1, 136
gremolata with roast bone marrow
82, 187
grits, breakfast grits with
strawberries & maple syrup 40
guacamole, boozy 126–7, 185

H

ham 80
green eggs & ham 33
ham, pesto & mozzarella pasta
bake 94
pesto, ricotta & Parma ham bagel
pizzas 79
honeycomb crunch refrigerator
squares 144

I

ice cream terrine, rocky road 157
ice lollies, boozy smoothie 166–7
iced tea, Earl Grey 171

K

kale 53
crunchy pesto-baked salmon with
blackened kale 100–1

L

lamb, spiced lamb patties with light
tzatziki & pitta bread 131, 180
lasagne, frying-pan 95, 180
latkes, smoked salmon latkes with
lemon crème fraîche, chopped red
onion & capers 44–5
lemon 88
Dutch baby pancake with 38
lemon crème fraîche 44–5
lemon honey 41
lemon posset 165, 186
thyme lemonade 172–3
lime
lime cheesecake cups 155, 185
soured cream & lime dressing 61,
69, 70
limoncello & raspberry Victoria
sandwich 152–3

M

mackerel 103
easy smoked mackerel pâté 81, 187
mackerel mayo & quick pickled
cucumber sandwiches 65
margarita, classic 171
mayo, pesto 62
miso soup, quick late night 110
mojito, brown sugar 175
moules marinière, classic 119
mozzarella 95, 105
ham, pesto & mozzarella pasta
bake 94
muffins
banana & Nutella 146
blueberry & oat breakfast 39
mulled wine 177
mushroom 46–7, 53, 97, 110, 140–1
mushrooms on toast with tamago
ribbons 84
pea, prawn & mushroom egg fried
rice 111
ten-minute mushrooms & bacon
on toast 85, 187

N

noodles
Asian prawn noodle salad with
crunchy greens 54–5
chicken noodle & oyster sauce
stir-fry 113
cold & crunchy winter vegetable
noodle salad with Asian
Dressing 53
pad Thai 112
Nutella
banana & Nutella muffins 146
easy Nutella cheesecake cups 154,
185

O

onion gravy 120–1, 136
orange 58, 176, 177
orange chocolate chip cookies 145
rhubarb, orange & ginger crumble
161
oyster sauce & chicken noodle
stir-fry 113

P

pad Thai 112
pancakes
  autumn-spiced banana pancakes 37
  classic Dutch baby pancake with
    lemon & sugar 38
  overnight buttermilk pancakes 36
pasta
  blistered cherry tomato
    puttanesca 92
  frozen seafood & white wine
    linguini 91
  frying-pan lasagne 95
  grated courgette pasta 88
  ham, pesto & mozzarella pasta
    bake 94
  the only tuna pasta salad you'll
    ever need 57
  pasta in tomato, tuna & caper
    sauce 90, 183
  roasted vegetable pasta 93
  tinned tomato pasta sauce 89, 187
  warm leftover roast chicken honey
    mustard pasta salad 52, 180
pâté, easy smoked mackerel 81, 187
patties, spiced lamb patties with light
  tzatziki & pitta bread 131
pea, prawn & mushroom egg fried
  rice 111
pearl barley, pomegranate &
  pistachio salad 50
pepper 14, 66, 76, 93, 125, 126–7, 132
  roasted red peppers with
    tomatoes & anchovies 118
pesto
ham, pesto & mozzarella pasta
  bake 94
pesto, ricotta & Parma ham bagel
  pizzas 79
  pesto mayo 62
  tuna & pesto rice 99
Pico de Gallo salsa 34, 43, 126–7
pies
  leftover roast chicken 140–1
  sweet potato sausage shepherd's
    137
pilchards on toast 68, 183

pitta bread 75
  light tzatziki with home-baked
    pitta chips 78
  pork souvlaki with light tzatziki &
    pitta bread 130
pizza
  pesto, ricotta & Parma ham bagel
    pizzas 79
  twice-cooked pizza baked potato
    105
pomegranate, pistachio & pearl
barley salad 50
pork souvlaki with light tzatziki &
pitta bread 130
potato 44, 76, 103, 133
  Cajun potato wedges 106–7
  Indian spiced potatoes 83, 187
  leftover baked Indian-spiced
    potatoes with tomato, egg &
    coriander 28
  mustard mash 120
  the only potato salad recipe you'll
    ever need 56
  twice-cooked pizza baked potato
    105, 180
  za'atar potatoes 138–9, 180, 186
prawn 112
  Asian prawn noodle salad with
    crunchy greens 54–5
  Cajun prawn tacos 70–1
  pea, prawn & mushroom egg fried
    rice 111
pumpkin & coconut soup 98
puttanesca, blistered cherry tomato
  92

Q

quiche, full English breakfast 46–7

R

raspberry
  chocolate ganache & fresh
    raspberry tart 158
  raspberry & limoncello Victoria
    sandwich 152–3

rhubarb
  forced rhubarb & cardamom
    breakfast compote 22
  rhubarb, orange & ginger crumble
    161
rice 15, 72, 97
  pea, prawn & mushroom egg fried
    rice 111
  rainbow sprinkle Rice Krispie
    treats 151
  seafood citrus salad rice bowl 58
  tuna & pesto rice 99
ricotta
  pesto, ricotta & Parma ham bagel
    pizzas 79
  strawberry & ricotta breakfast
    toast with lemon honey 41
rocky road ice cream terrine 157, 183
rum
  brown sugar mojito 175
  rum-spiked banana bread 147

S

salads
  Asian prawn noodle salad with
    crunchy greens 54–5
  BLTA chopped salad with skinny
    buttermilk ranch dressing 60, 182
  cold & crunchy winter vegetable
    noodle salad with Asian
    Dressing 53
  fattoush 75
  Israeli chopped mixed bean salad 59
  leftover bread panzanella salad 73
  loaded fajita salad with soured
    cream & lime dressing 69
  the only potato salad recipe you'll
    ever need 56
  pearl barley, pomegranate &
    pistachio salad 50
  seafood citrus salad rice bowl 58
  warm leftover roast chicken honey
    mustard pasta salad 52, 180
salmon
  crunchy pesto-baked salmon with
    blackened kale 100–1

hot salmon & avocado salad with
soured cream & lime dressing 61
smoked salmon bagel breakfast
casserole 26–7, 182
smoked salmon latkes with lemon
crème fraîche, chopped red
onion & capers 44–5, 182
salsa, Pico de Gallo 34, 43, 126–7
sandwiches
devilled egg 64
leftover roast chicken, pesto mayo
& tomato 62
mackerel mayo & quick pickled
cucumber 65
sangria, classic 176
sausage 46–7
sausage bolognese 95, 134–5, 137,
180, 184
sausage roast with mustard
soured cream 122–3
sausages with mustard mash &
onion gravy 120–1
suped-up sausage rolls 80
sweet potato sausage shepherd's
pie 137
toad in the hole with onion gravy
136
schnitzel, chicken schnitzel with
capers, anchovies & a fried egg 108–9
seafood
frozen seafood & white wine
linguini 91
seafood citrus salad rice bowl 58
shepherd's pie, sweet potato
sausage 137
smoothie boozy ice lollies 166
soup
a basic chicken 97
carrot 96
quick & creamy pumpkin &
coconut 98, 182
quick late night miso 110
souvlaki, pork souvlaki with light
tzatziki & pitta bread 130
spinach, yoghurt & berries with
granola 20–1
steak, sharing steak with thyme-
roasted cherry tomatoes 116–17, 186

stir-fry, chicken noodle & oyster
sauce 113
strawberry 176
breakfast grits with strawberries &
maple syrup 40
strawberry & ricotta breakfast
toast with lemon honey 41
white wine-soaked strawberries
164, 186
sweet potato 124
lighter tuna & sweetcorn baked
sweet potato 104
sweet potato sausage shepherd's
pie 137
sweetcorn 57
lighter tuna & sweetcorn baked
sweet potato 104

T
tacos, Cajun prawn 70–1
tart, chocolate ganache & fresh
raspberry 158
tea, Earl Grey iced 171
thyme lemonade 172–3
toad in the hole with onion gravy 136
toast
chicken liver & onions on toast 30
mushrooms on toast with tamago
ribbons 84
pilchards on toast 68, 183
strawberry & ricotta breakfast
toast with lemon honey 41
ten-minute mushrooms & bacon
on toast 85
tomato 24, 46–7, 52, 59–60, 73, 75,
132–4
blistered cherry tomato
puttanesca 92
BLTA chopped salad with skinny
buttermilk ranch dressing 60, 182
leftover baked Indian-spiced
potatoes with tomato, egg &
coriander 28
leftover roast chicken, pesto mayo
& tomato sandwich 62
pasta in tomato, tuna & caper
sauce 90, 183

roasted red peppers with
tomatoes & anchovies 118
sharing steak with thyme-roasted
cherry tomatoes 116–17
single-serving spicy baked eggs in
tomato sauce 31
tinned tomato pasta sauce 89, 187
tortillas 43, 66–7, 69–72, 126–7
tuna 103
lighter tuna & sweetcorn baked
sweet potato 104
the only tuna pasta salad you'll
ever need 57
pasta in tomato, tuna & caper
sauce 90, 183
tuna & pesto rice 99, 183, 187
tzatziki, light 78, 180

V
Victoria sandwich cake, raspberry
& limoncello 152–3

W
Welsh rarebit 63
wraps
bacon & avocado 67
super veggie rainbow 66

ACKNOWLEDGEMENTS

First, I want to thank my amazing literary agent Diana Beaumont. This book would never have happened if you had not decided that I had a story worth telling, and fought to be the one to help me tell it. I could not ask for a better champion.

While I may have supplied the words and pictures, this book would just be a word document and a load of images if it were not for the team at Ebury, especially my wonderful editor Laura Higginson, and Lucy Harrison in production. Also, I want to give a massive thank you to Louise Evans and Two Associates for helping to make this book look so fantastic, inside and out, and to Kay Delves and Kate Parker for their help in making sure my words put their best foot forward.

Writing this book is probably the hardest thing I have ever done, and I know I would never have managed without you, Daddy and Womble. For all of the trips to the supermarket for ingredients, for all of the washing and clearing up, for eating all of my experiments (whether they've been successful or not!) and for picking me up all of those times when left to my own devises, I probably would have given up surrounded by piles of dirty dishes and plates of food I was finding it impossible to photograph. I will never be able to thank you both enough for all that you've done for me.

Jon, for every single time you've read through my manuscripts, looked over proofs and given me real feedback, and not just told me what I wanted to hear. And for always being there, even when sometimes I haven't deserved it.

To all of my friends and colleagues who have helped me test recipes for this book (and again, for putting up with me while I wrote it, trying everything without complaint!), especially Ed, Eddie, Kathryn, Sherin and Elle.

Charlie, thank you for letting me have the time to write and photograph this book when many other people wouldn't have done. You had faith in me, taught me how to be a team player and made me a better person for it.

Natasha, Henry and Nicole, for all of your help right in the beginning helping me with pitches and proposals, giving me feedback and proof-reading everything.

And finally, thank you to everyone who clicks through and reads my blog every day. Without you, they probably would have never asked me to write this book in the first place.

1 3 5 7 9 10 8 6 4 2

Ebury Press, an imprint of Ebury Publishing,
20 Vauxhall Bridge Road,
London, SW1V 2SA

Ebury Press is part of the Penguin Random House group of companies whose addresses can be found at global.penguinrandomhouse.com

Penguin
Random House
UK

First published by Ebury Press in 2017

www.penguin.co.uk

A CIP catalogue record for this book is available from the British Library

Design: Louise Evans

ISBN: 978-1-785-03366-7

Printed and bound in China by C&C Offset Co Ltd

Colour Orignation by Born Group, London, UK

Penguin Random House is committed to a sustainable future for our business, our readers and our planet. This book is made from Forest Stewardship Council® certified